LOVE AND A WOODEN SPOON

LOVE AND A WOODEN SPOON

Charmaine Solomon

Recipes,
anecdotes and poems
to bring happiness to the heart
of young and old.
With a special celebration menu
and suggestions for Christmas,
Birthdays and Holidays.

illustrations by Dee Huxley

Doubleday & Company, Inc.
Garden City, New York
1984

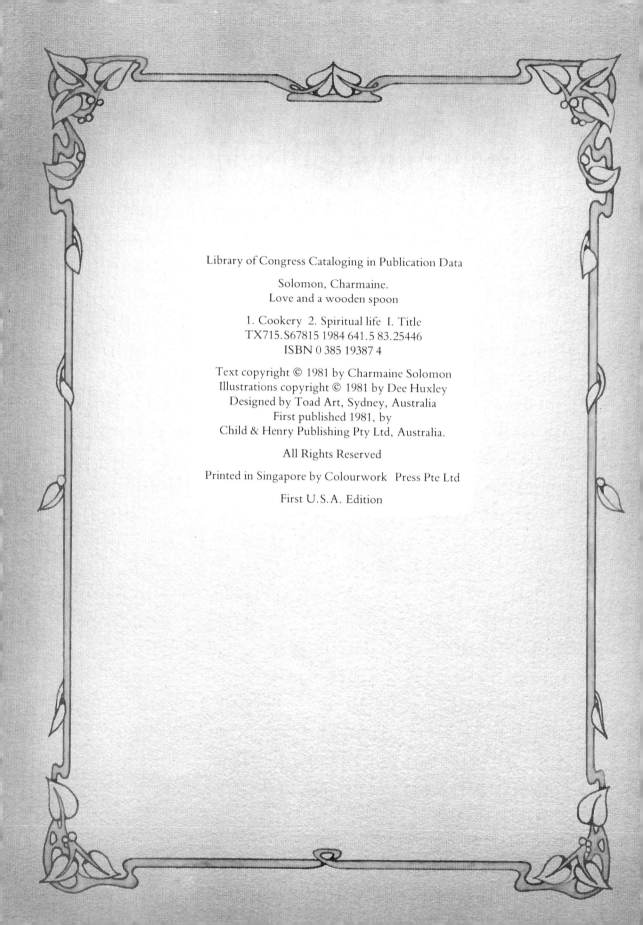

Library of Congress Cataloging in Publication Data

Solomon, Charmaine.
Love and a wooden spoon

1. Cookery 2. Spiritual life I. Title
TX715.S67815 1984 641.5 83.25446
ISBN 0 385 19387 4

Text copyright © 1981 by Charmaine Solomon
Illustrations copyright © 1981 by Dee Huxley
Designed by Toad Art, Sydney, Australia
First published 1981, by
Child & Henry Publishing Pty Ltd, Australia.

Printed in Singapore by Colourwork Press Pte Ltd

First U.S.A. Edition

To those who have filled my life with love

CONTENTS

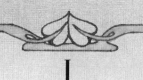

I
ABOUT THIS BOOK

A poetry book with recipes? A cookery book with poems? A little of both, I suppose. But more than anything, it is a memory book. Not just my memory book, but yours too, for there are pages specially reserved for you.

Ever since I was a little girl I've been scribbling poems. It was my way of turning inside out, something we all need to do once in a while. The poems are very simple, as you can see, inspired (if that is not too grand a word) by the everyday things that happen to almost every woman.

Marriage, a home and a family were the catalysts for some of my best efforts—or, at any rate, those that still give me the most pleasure as they recall moments all too fleeting. But that new life also cut down the time available to sit, pen in hand, committing to paper all the thoughts and feelings I would have liked to record.

I once wrote to my husband:

> I wish I could let you know, my love,
> what joy you've brought my way.
> There doesn't seem to be the time
> to find the things to say.
> Instead of a sonnet, a mended shirt
> (but it leaves so much unsaid);
> instead of a love song, the cup of tea
> I bring to you in bed.
> I wish I could say it with flourish and pomp
> as they did in days of yore,
> but our time-saving, built-in, push-button world
> leaves us less time than before . . . . .

But poems do not fill the stomach—and *that*, as every wife learns early in marriage, is of prime importance. So I found a more practical way to express myself. Enjoying every minute of it, I learned to cook. Not at a school, but by trial and error in my own kitchen.

Cooking is no less an act of love than writing a sonnet. Just because the results of those hours of effort vanish without a trace (except for dishes to be washed), it doesn't mean to say they're not appreciated and remembered. I really love to cook for family and friends.

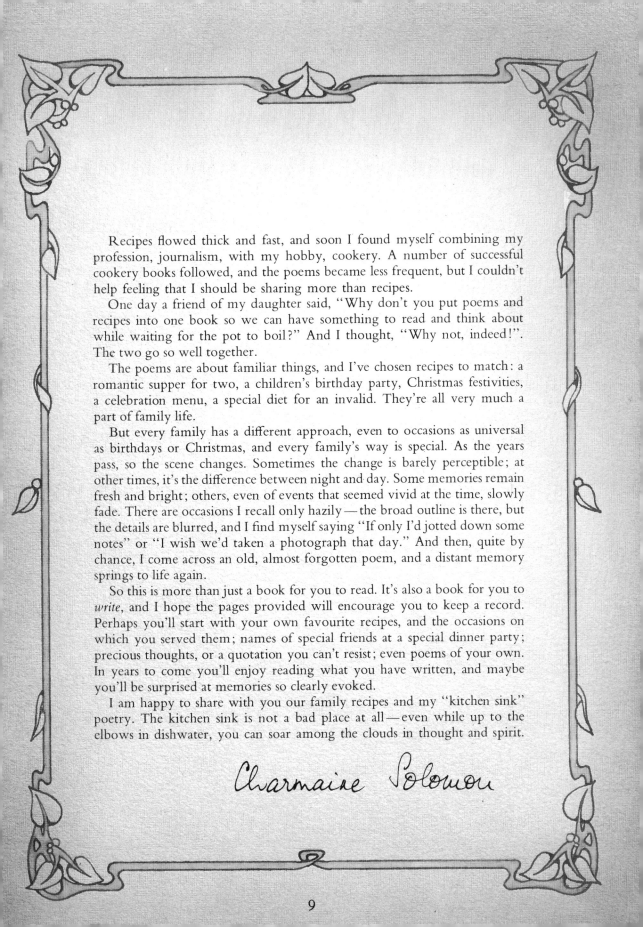

Recipes flowed thick and fast, and soon I found myself combining my profession, journalism, with my hobby, cookery. A number of successful cookery books followed, and the poems became less frequent, but I couldn't help feeling that I should be sharing more than recipes.

One day a friend of my daughter said, "Why don't you put poems and recipes into one book so we can have something to read and think about while waiting for the pot to boil?" And I thought, "Why not, indeed!". The two go so well together.

The poems are about familiar things, and I've chosen recipes to match: a romantic supper for two, a children's birthday party, Christmas festivities, a celebration menu, a special diet for an invalid. They're all very much a part of family life.

But every family has a different approach, even to occasions as universal as birthdays or Christmas, and every family's way is special. As the years pass, so the scene changes. Sometimes the change is barely perceptible; at other times, it's the difference between night and day. Some memories remain fresh and bright; others, even of events that seemed vivid at the time, slowly fade. There are occasions I recall only hazily — the broad outline is there, but the details are blurred, and I find myself saying "If only I'd jotted down some notes" or "I wish we'd taken a photograph that day." And then, quite by chance, I come across an old, almost forgotten poem, and a distant memory springs to life again.

So this is more than just a book for you to read. It's also a book for you to *write*, and I hope the pages provided will encourage you to keep a record. Perhaps you'll start with your own favourite recipes, and the occasions on which you served them; names of special friends at a special dinner party; precious thoughts, or a quotation you can't resist; even poems of your own. In years to come you'll enjoy reading what you have written, and maybe you'll be surprised at memories so clearly evoked.

I am happy to share with you our family recipes and my "kitchen sink" poetry. The kitchen sink is not a bad place at all — even while up to the elbows in dishwater, you can soar among the clouds in thought and spirit.

Charmaine Solomon

Today and Tomorrow

Dear Lord,
if only I could still the hands of time,
stop them just where they are right now,
and hold the world in a beautiful golden bubble,
a place where nothing changes.

Well, maybe some things could be better.
We'd like to have more time together
and not have to work so hard, so long,
to pay the bills and keep things going.
But I don't expect perfection.
And you have blessed us
with strength and willingness to work.
You have blessed us with children;
help us enjoy them and not only spend our time
training them, bringing them up right.
You have blessed us with love for each other;
after all these years there is still
the fun of jokes shared,
the benediction of tenderness,
the flame of desire.

Yes, Lord, I love my life.
I thank you for this gift that embraces all gifts.
Take from me the fear of change,
give me faith to believe not only with my head
but with my heart
that your mercies are from everlasting to everlasting.
May I let the clock of life move on
unafraid,
knowing the time ahead is in your hands
just like the years before.

II
NEW YEAR

I love people and parties, and have been known to initiate some good gatherings myself, but I've never been comfortable at a New Year's Eve party. I suppose the experiences of childhood have a big part to play in adult attitudes, and my instincts at this time have been shaped by years of greeting the New Year at a watchnight service and coming home after midnight (in itself a big event in my young life). There on the dining table, high and golden-brown and still faintly warm from the oven, was the large *breudher*—a rich, fragrant yeast cake baked in a fluted mould, the first thing we tasted in the New Year. The family sat around and ate slices of the light, buttery cake accompanied by thin slivers of sharp Dutch Edam cut from the big ball of cheese with its coating of shiny red wax. This was as predictable as the dawn, and is a tradition I have managed to preserve in my own family even in a faraway land.

On New Year's Eve I really like being at home in the quiet of my kitchen, up to the wrists in flour. I just have this feeling that it's a good way to start the year, doing something as basic and comforting as making bread. As I knead and mix and bake I get to thinking that in spite of the gloomy headlines and the unpredictability of life in general, nothing is going to happen that, with God's help, I can't handle.

The dough is baked into *breudher*, not only for ourselves but for friends and neighbours as well. It is my version of the *breudher* of my childhood, a Dutch recipe that used twenty egg yolks and was beaten by hand by the most stalwart member of the family. I'm a traditionalist at heart, and it was no arbitrary whim that made me change the recipe, but apart from not being able to afford twenty yolks when we were a struggling young family, I didn't really want twenty egg whites reproaching me every time I opened the fridge!

So I adapted. And I tried it out on friends from my own country. When they approved, I was elated. And when my oldest and best friend, herself a good cook, says she now uses my recipe and loves the result, then I know nothing has been lost in the translation.

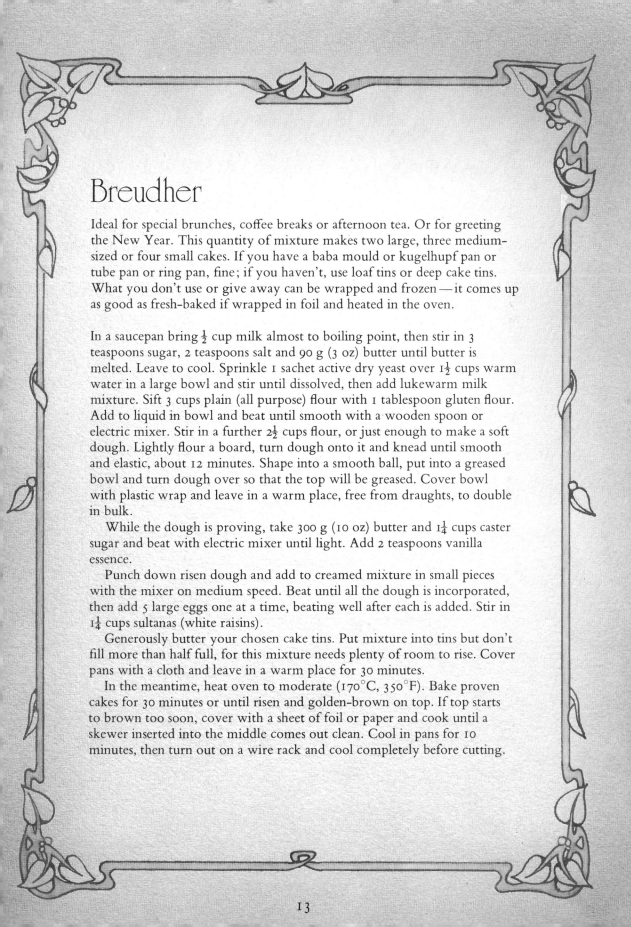

Breudher

Ideal for special brunches, coffee breaks or afternoon tea. Or for greeting
the New Year. This quantity of mixture makes two large, three medium-
sized or four small cakes. If you have a baba mould or kugelhupf pan or
tube pan or ring pan, fine; if you haven't, use loaf tins or deep cake tins.
What you don't use or give away can be wrapped and frozen—it comes up
as good as fresh-baked if wrapped in foil and heated in the oven.

In a saucepan bring $\frac{1}{2}$ cup milk almost to boiling point, then stir in 3
teaspoons sugar, 2 teaspoons salt and 90 g (3 oz) butter until butter is
melted. Leave to cool. Sprinkle 1 sachet active dry yeast over $1\frac{1}{2}$ cups warm
water in a large bowl and stir until dissolved, then add lukewarm milk
mixture. Sift 3 cups plain (all purpose) flour with 1 tablespoon gluten flour.
Add to liquid in bowl and beat until smooth with a wooden spoon or
electric mixer. Stir in a further $2\frac{1}{2}$ cups flour, or just enough to make a soft
dough. Lightly flour a board, turn dough onto it and knead until smooth
and elastic, about 12 minutes. Shape into a smooth ball, put into a greased
bowl and turn dough over so that the top will be greased. Cover bowl
with plastic wrap and leave in a warm place, free from draughts, to double
in bulk.

   While the dough is proving, take 300 g (10 oz) butter and $1\frac{1}{4}$ cups caster
sugar and beat with electric mixer until light. Add 2 teaspoons vanilla
essence.

   Punch down risen dough and add to creamed mixture in small pieces
with the mixer on medium speed. Beat until all the dough is incorporated,
then add 5 large eggs one at a time, beating well after each is added. Stir in
$1\frac{1}{4}$ cups sultanas (white raisins).

   Generously butter your chosen cake tins. Put mixture into tins but don't
fill more than half full, for this mixture needs plenty of room to rise. Cover
pans with a cloth and leave in a warm place for 30 minutes.

   In the meantime, heat oven to moderate (170°C, 350°F). Bake proven
cakes for 30 minutes or until risen and golden-brown on top. If top starts
to brown too soon, cover with a sheet of foil or paper and cook until a
skewer inserted into the middle comes out clean. Cool in pans for 10
minutes, then turn out on a wire rack and cool completely before cutting.

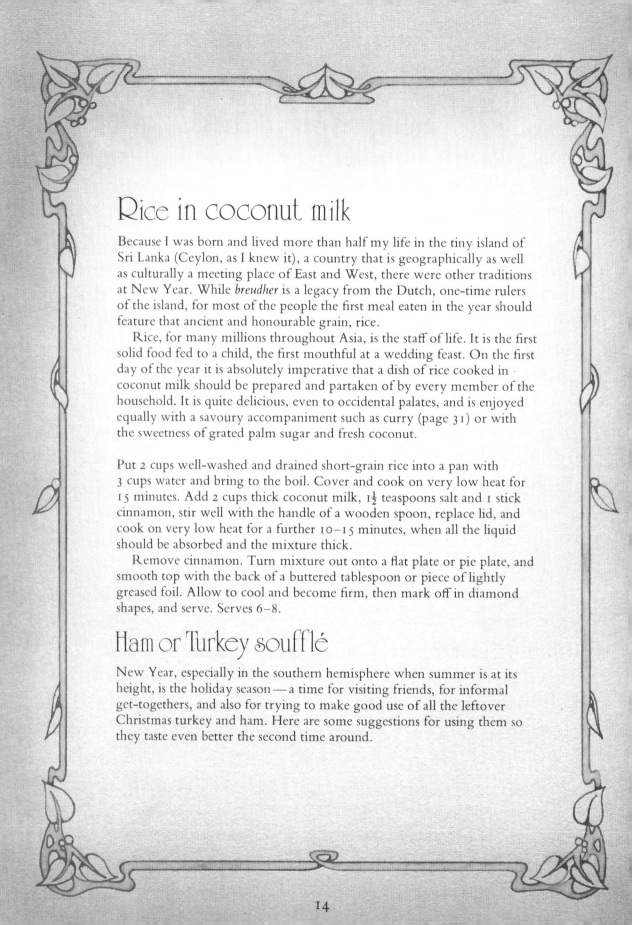

Rice in coconut milk

Because I was born and lived more than half my life in the tiny island of Sri Lanka (Ceylon, as I knew it), a country that is geographically as well as culturally a meeting place of East and West, there were other traditions at New Year. While *breudher* is a legacy from the Dutch, one-time rulers of the island, for most of the people the first meal eaten in the year should feature that ancient and honourable grain, rice.

Rice, for many millions throughout Asia, is the staff of life. It is the first solid food fed to a child, the first mouthful at a wedding feast. On the first day of the year it is absolutely imperative that a dish of rice cooked in coconut milk should be prepared and partaken of by every member of the household. It is quite delicious, even to occidental palates, and is enjoyed equally with a savoury accompaniment such as curry (page 31) or with the sweetness of grated palm sugar and fresh coconut.

Put 2 cups well-washed and drained short-grain rice into a pan with 3 cups water and bring to the boil. Cover and cook on very low heat for 15 minutes. Add 2 cups thick coconut milk, 1½ teaspoons salt and 1 stick cinnamon, stir well with the handle of a wooden spoon, replace lid, and cook on very low heat for a further 10–15 minutes, when all the liquid should be absorbed and the mixture thick.

Remove cinnamon. Turn mixture out onto a flat plate or pie plate, and smooth top with the back of a buttered tablespoon or piece of lightly greased foil. Allow to cool and become firm, then mark off in diamond shapes, and serve. Serves 6–8.

Ham or Turkey soufflé

New Year, especially in the southern hemisphere when summer is at its height, is the holiday season — a time for visiting friends, for informal get-togethers, and also for trying to make good use of all the leftover Christmas turkey and ham. Here are some suggestions for using them so they taste even better the second time around.

Preheat oven to hot (200°C, 400°F). Melt 60 g (2 oz) butter in a heavy saucepan and cook 4 finely chopped spring onions over low heat until soft and golden. Add 3 tablespoons plain (all purpose) flour and cook, stirring, for a minute or two without browning. Add 1¼ cups hot milk and whisk over low heat until thick and smooth. Turn off heat, season sauce with 1 teaspoon dry mustard, and salt and pepper to taste.

Add the yolks of 4 eggs one at a time, beating well after each is added. Stir in 1 cup finely chopped or minced turkey or ham. Beat egg whites with a pinch of salt and cream of tartar until they hold stiff peaks, stir a third of the egg whites into the sauce mixture to lighten it, then gently and lightly fold in the remaining egg whites.

Pour into a five- or six-cup soufflé dish which has been greased with butter and dusted with dry breadcrumbs. Put into the hot oven, then turn heat down to moderately hot (190°C, 375°F) and bake for 30 minutes or until soufflé is risen high and golden-brown on top. Serve at once. Serves 6 as an entrée, 3 or 4 as a main course.

Turkey or Ham Crêpes: Make a batch of crêpes using the recipe on page 134. Make cream sauce (page 135), fold in 3 cups finely chopped ham or turkey, add a dash of hot pepper sauce or mustard, about 1 cup finely diced celery, a little grated onion, and season to taste with salt and pepper. Use this as a filling for the crêpes, roll up and place in a buttered heatproof dish. Heat through in the oven, or serve cold.

Savoury Choux Puffs: Make some bite-sized choux pastry puffs using the recipe for Gougère (page 124), but omitting the cheese. Bake by small teaspoonfuls, and when done split on one side and fill with the same savoury mixture as for crêpes (above). Serve hot or cold.

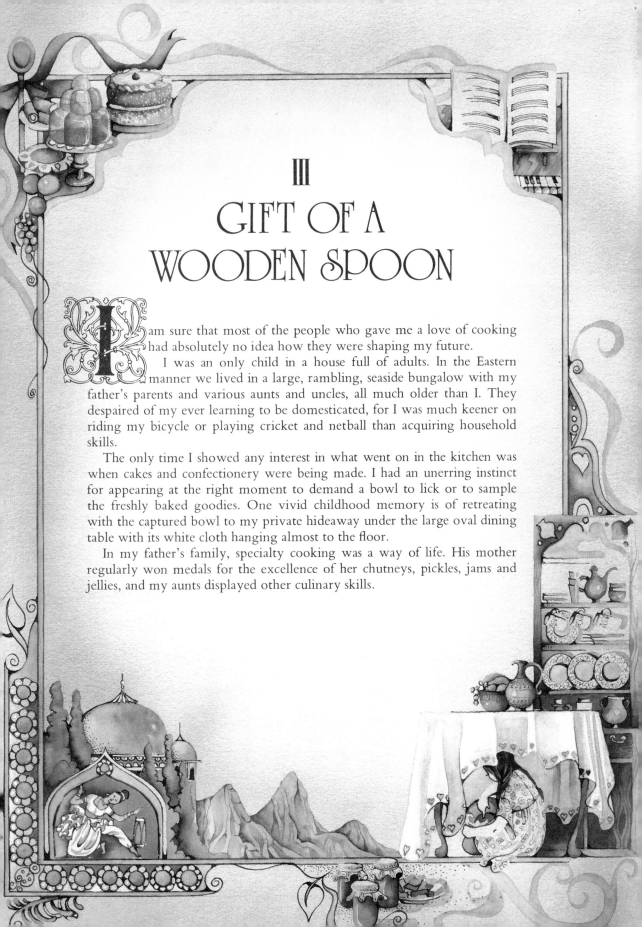

III
GIFT OF A
WOODEN SPOON

I am sure that most of the people who gave me a love of cooking had absolutely no idea how they were shaping my future.

I was an only child in a house full of adults. In the Eastern manner we lived in a large, rambling, seaside bungalow with my father's parents and various aunts and uncles, all much older than I. They despaired of my ever learning to be domesticated, for I was much keener on riding my bicycle or playing cricket and netball than acquiring household skills.

The only time I showed any interest in what went on in the kitchen was when cakes and confectionery were being made. I had an unerring instinct for appearing at the right moment to demand a bowl to lick or to sample the freshly baked goodies. One vivid childhood memory is of retreating with the captured bowl to my private hideaway under the large oval dining table with its white cloth hanging almost to the floor.

In my father's family, specialty cooking was a way of life. His mother regularly won medals for the excellence of her chutneys, pickles, jams and jellies, and my aunts displayed other culinary skills.

Most skilled in the art of confectionery, cakes and similar sweet things was my Aunt Muriel. As a child, I called her "Moonie", and that was what she was lovingly called for ever after — not just by me, but by everyone in the family. She was in her forties when I was born, but as I grew up she was my confidante and friend in spite of the difference in our ages.

At first it was cupboard love, pure and simple. I was drawn to this tall, gentle person who left extra cake batter in the bowl for me. She always seemed to have around her a fragrance of vanilla, and that to me meant good things to eat. She also had a wonderful gift for music, and played the piano with as much flair as she created good food.

Moonie spent a great deal of time preparing delicacies for anyone who was sick — friends, neighbours, acquaintances. I recall the hours of simmering needed for calf's foot jelly (in those days highly regarded as a great strengthener for convalescents), and the transparent layers of another kind of jelly made from sea moss that took days to prepare. At least twenty-four hours of repeated soaking and cleaning were necessary before the simmering, clarifying and flavouring could be started. The love that went with her offerings was the best medicine of all — she would take the food to the patients herself, sit with them, cheer them up, read to them.

She also made the most delicious coconut ice. Melt-in-the-mouth is the only way to describe it, and it spoiled all other kinds of coconut ice for me. Other people simply used grated coconut, but she took freshly grated coconut meat and ground it on a large stone slab until the particles were as fine as almond meal. Only then did she cook the coconut in a syrup of refined sugar and colour it delicately pink or green.

Waiting in a kitchen for tidbits is a pleasant way to learn the rules of cooking, and almost unconsciously I was absorbing elementary wisdom: egg whites must go into an absolutely clean, grease-free bowl or they will not whip up; flour must be sifted three times for the lightest cakes. (From the dim past comes an echo, "No, no, *no*! You don't pat it down flat after it has been sifted, that takes all the air out of it." There must be something irresistible about a white mountain of freshly sifted flour, for I had to restrain *my* children from doing exactly the same thing.)

My mother has the sweetest tooth of all time, and she used to make a delicious creamy fudge that I've since made many a time for my own brood. I loved watching as the mixture bubbled thickly, reaching that critical soft-ball stage which only experience teaches you to gauge (unless there is a sugar thermometer handy). When fudge is beaten, too, experience is necessary to know just when to stop beating and pour it into the dish which is buttered, ready and waiting. No time to fiddle around then, or the fudge will lose its gloss and become dry and crumbly.

When I was older I learnt a great deal from Nana, my mother's mother. She had lived in Burma all her life, surrounded by every comfort. Then World War II came. For weeks Nana endured the nightmare of bombings and invasion before joining thousands of her countrymen in a month-long trek to India and safety. She was in her fifties, and suffered incredible hardships as she struggled across swollen rivers and through leech-infested jungles to reach, at the end of that awful journey, the austerities of a refugee camp — such a far cry from her lovely home, but when she came to live with us after the war there was no bitterness in her at all.

Her stories of long ago were fascinating, though she was not one to sit with folded hands, re-living the past. No, indeed. Her approach to life was active, practical, completely capable. She held my family together when, as a young mother with three children under five years (including a new baby), I sent her an SOS to come halfway across the world to live with us. She arrived when the baby was three weeks old, and made him her special project.

She died five years later, but what a lot we had learned from her about courage and faith. Yes, and recipes too . . . recipes from Burma and India that I would not otherwise have had the chance to know.

My kitchen is usually a hive of activity, yet even when I'm alone there I am anything but lonely. I have so many memories of those people in my past who started me on a life-long love affair with good cooking.

Aunt Elva's date cake

Set oven temperature at moderate (170°C, 350°F). Grease two 20 cm (8 inch) sandwich pans.

Chop 250 g (8 oz) dates very finely or put through a mincer. Dissolve 1 teaspoon baking soda (bicarbonate of soda) in 1 cup boiling water, pour over dates and leave to cool. (You may like to add 1 teaspoon instant coffee to the hot water — it gives the cake a subtle oomph.)

Cream 250 g (8 oz) butter and 1 cup sugar until light and fluffy, then add 3 eggs one at a time, beating well after each is added. Stir in soaked date mixture with 1 teaspoon vanilla essence and fold in 2 cups plain (all purpose) flour, pour into prepared pans and bake in a moderate oven for about 35 minutes.

When cakes are completely cooled, ice with **Coffee Frosting**: Cream 125 g (4 oz) butter and 1½ cups icing sugar. Add 1 egg, and 2 teaspoons instant coffee powder dissolved in 2 teaspoons hot water and beat until light and creamy. A teaspoon of vanilla essence or rum may be added to frosting if liked.

Mum's easy fudge

Butter a square 20 cm (8 inch) pan or dish. In a heavy saucepan combine 410 g (14 oz) can sweetened condensed milk, ¾ cup milk, 1½ cups sugar and 60 g (2 oz) butter. Stir over medium heat until boiling and boil, stirring until it reaches the soft-ball stage. This will register 114°C (238°F) on a sugar thermometer; alternatively, drop a little of the mixture into a glass of iced water to see if it forms a soft ball. Remove pan from the heat while testing so mixture doesn't overcook. Let mixture cool slightly, then add 2 teaspoons vanilla essence and beat until fudge thickens and just starts to lose its gloss. Quickly pour into buttered dish. When firm, cut into squares with a sharp knife.

Chocolate velvet cake

How I loved helping Moonie make this cake, even though the creaming of butter and sugar (in the days before electric mixers!) was enough to make my arm ache. I was all for cutting short the hard work, but she kept going until a speck of the mixture, dropped into a cup of cold water, would float instead of sinking to the bottom. That is the test of a well-creamed mixture.

Grease and flour a 20 cm (8 inch) cake tin, line base with greaseproof paper and brush the paper with melted butter. Sift 6 level tablespoons of cocoa into a small bowl, pressing out any lumps. Gradually add $\frac{1}{4}$ cup evaporated milk and mix to a smooth paste. In a small saucepan heat $\frac{1}{2}$ cup evaporated milk to boiling, then pour it slowly over the cocoa, stirring. Return to saucepan and cook over low heat, stirring constantly, until smooth and slightly thick. Set aside to cool. Sift $1\frac{1}{2}$ cups plain (all purpose) flour. Add $4\frac{1}{2}$ tablespoons cornflour and 1 teaspoon cream of tartar and sift twice more. Dissolve $\frac{1}{2}$ teaspoon baking soda (bicarbonate of soda) in $\frac{1}{2}$ cup cold water.

Preheat oven to moderate ($170°$C, $350°$F).

Cream 125 g (4 oz) butter softened at room temperature and $1\frac{1}{2}$ cups caster sugar until light. Separate yolks and whites of 3 small- to medium-sized eggs and add the yolks one at a time to the creamed mixture, beating well after each is added. Add the water/soda mixture a teaspoon at a time, beating well. Mix in cocoa and 1 teaspoon vanilla essence. Beat egg whites with a whisk or rotary beater until they hold stiff peaks but are not dry.

If you have been using an electric mixer up to this point, stop now. This is when you should use a spatula. Fold egg whites into batter alternately with the sifted flour, gently but thoroughly. You'll find this is a very liquid batter. Pour into prepared cake tin and bake in a moderate oven for 1 hour or until a fine skewer inserted into the centre comes out clean. Cover with foil or brown paper if top starts to brown too soon. Cool in tin for 10 minutes, then turn out on wire rack and allow to get quite cold.

If you prefer a filled cake, cook the mixture in two sandwich pans for about 35 minutes or until they test "done" — you know, slight shrinking away from the edge of the pan with the top springing back when lightly touched, or use the old reliable skewer test.

This is a moist, good-keeping cake, and deserves a rich chocolate frosting.

Love cake

This chapter would not be complete without a mention of my mother's sister, Connie. As a young woman I went to live with her for a few months in one of the beautiful garden counties of England while I attended college in a nearby city. It was during this visit that we really got to know each other, and she increased my love of cooking through her creative and confident approach.

Her children were then adorable little girls, six and three years old respectively, but are now young mothers with children of their own, and to my joy I was recently able to visit them again. Connie and Alison, the younger daughter, were having their birthdays that week so I took with me, all the way from Australia, an offering of a special cake that is the traditional birthday cake in Sri Lanka and bears the intriguing name of Love Cake. There are many recipes, all differing slightly. This is the one my mother makes.

Put 375 g (12 oz) semolina (farina) into a heavy frying pan and place over medium heat, stirring constantly or shaking pan until semolina is toasted a pale biscuit colour. Remove from pan and allow to cool.

Prepare a 22.5 cm (9 inch) square cake tin, lining it with two thicknesses of brown paper and one of greaseproof paper. Brush paper with melted butter. Set oven temperature at low (120°C, 250°F).

In large bowl of electric mixer beat 3 whole eggs and 2 extra yolks (reserve egg whites) with 500 g (1 lb) caster sugar and the finely chopped rind of a green lime or lemon until light and creamy. Add ½ teaspoon each of ground cinnamon, cloves, cardamom and grated nutmeg, and mix well. Add 2 tablespoons each of rosewater, brandy and honey, and mix again. Gradually mix in ½ cup evaporated milk.

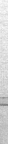

Stir in 250 g (8 oz) very finely chopped raw cashew nuts, 1 tablespoon soft butter and the semolina, mixing thoroughly. Whip the 2 reserved egg whites until stiff and fold in. Pour into the prepared cake tin and sprinkle the top of the cake with 1 tablespoon extra caster sugar.

Bake in a slow oven for 2–2½ hours, covering top of cake halfway through baking with foil or paper to prevent it browning too much. Allow cake to cool in the tin. Cut into small squares to serve.

This very rich cake is intended to have a soft, moist centre, so if you're trying it for the first time don't think it is undercooked. Well wrapped, it keeps for weeks.

Note: If raw (natural) cashew nuts are not available, blanched almonds can be used instead. It is important that the nuts should be finely chopped, not ground.

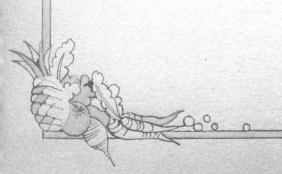

IV
STARTING OUT
and
STARTING OVER

Our early married life was the sort of ideal existence most people dream about. For the first three years we lived in a luxury hotel on a tropical island where my husband was a member of the resident orchestra and I had no problems about housekeeping or cooking or paying bills. Food and lodging were all part of the contract, and we dined luxuriously on meals produced by French and Swiss chefs.

Why, you may ask, when we had it so good did we leave it all to make a new start in a foreign country? I suppose it's hard to believe, but all that ease and indulgence palled after a time, and we knew it was a very unreal life style. Besides, we wanted a home of our own, and the situation on the island was such that it was unwise for anyone who was not a national to make it a permanent home. So we made the big decision and sailed for Australia, complete with two babies and absolutely no idea of what it was going to be like, except that it would be very different. And different it was.

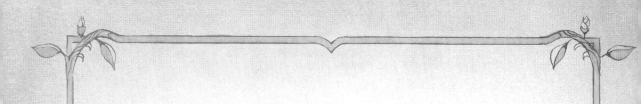

Having lived with my family until my marriage, I had never known the responsibility of running a home. In any case, the social structure in Ceylon at that time allowed for numerous servants to be part of every home — some who swept and cleaned, others who tended the garden, the *dhoby* who called each week with clean clothes and took away those that needed washing, the cook who only had to be told what the day's menus were and who then did all the marketing and cooking, and the *ayah* or children's nurse (top of the domestic hierarchy) whose only duty was to look after the children.

In our new life I had to learn a lot of skills, including simple housework. I learnt to cope with grocery shopping, and managed to make ends meet. And for the first time in my life I was totally responsible for our two girls, both under three years old and going through that terrible period when they are as quick as greased lightning and everything they do is potentially dangerous.

The money we brought over didn't go far at all, and we spent months looking for a house on which we could afford the down payment. Then, having got a loan, it looked as if we'd spend the rest of our lives paying it off.

But if I worked too, we could get out of debt faster. So I found work locally, choosing my positions in order to be home within minutes if the children needed me. Reuben minded them during the day, then I took over when he went off at night to his work as a musician. We seemed to be in a never-ending relay race, meeting only briefly as we swapped roles.

I worked with some nice people and found good friends. One of them gave me a wringer. She couldn't believe we had only an old copper in the laundry and wrung out the sheets and towels by hand, husband at one end and me at the other. But just having my own laundry was a joy indeed, for when we first arrived in Australia we had rented a room with nothing more than a sink and an old stove that must have come over with the First Fleet, and the rent was iniquitous.

The hardest thing I had to come to terms with was being alone. When I married and went to live in the hotel I had plenty of company. In rooms nearby were other orchestra wives, and we talked and played Scrabble and whiled away the hours when our husbands were playing for the guests.

When we moved into our house I was, quite literally, too scared to sleep until Reuben returned from work, generally about one o'clock in the morning. I was scared of being alone with just two toddlers for "protection". I was scared of burglars. I was scared of all the strange noises that houses make, and the experience of a possum in the roof sent me screaming for help to my long-suffering neighbour. I soon realised that sitting biting my nails after the children were asleep wouldn't help anything except a nervous breakdown.

So I started the hobby that was to become a very important part of my life. Cooking. I would lock every door, turn on all the lights and the radio, and cook furiously until Reuben returned. It would take a brave burglar to confront this crazy woman who cooked her way through the night, carving knives and rolling pins at hand!

The fringe benefits were tremendous. My husband had exciting suppers to come home to. I became quite a good cook, and actually looked forward to the long night hours.

All the knowledge I must have absorbed through watching my mother, grandmother and aunts started to surface. Of course there were gaps in my memory, so I would write home begging for this recipe or that, telling my problems, asking advice. Encouraged by Reuben I even entered a cookery contest run by a national magazine, and it was one of my biggest moments when I won a prize. This led to a position as a cookery journalist on the magazine, and so it went on, until a few years later I found myself working as a full-time author of cookery books.

But perhaps nothing equals the moment when I received a telegram of congratulations (for winning the contest) from my stunned family at home in Ceylon. Their tomboy, bookworm, career girl, had finally made it in the family tradition of cooking. She had started out and started over.

Here are some of my favourite recipes from those early days, including my prize-winning Cheese Daisies.

Cheese daisies

This quantity makes about 40 little biscuits with a delicious savoury flavour.
Popular at any time, they're especially good for serving with pre-dinner
drinks.

Toast 2 tablespoons sesame seeds in a dry frying pan over moderate heat
until golden. In a bowl cream together 185 g (6 oz) butter, 1½ cups grated
sharp Cheddar cheese and ¼ cup grated Parmesan cheese, then add toasted
sesame seeds. Sift 1½ cups plain (all purpose) flour with 1 teaspoon salt and
1 teaspoon paprika and add to creamed mixture. Mix well. Pile mixture
into a cookie press fitted with a flower disc, or a pastry tube with a large
star pipe. Press mixture out onto baking trays covered with ungreased foil.
Make tiny balls of the mixture, roll them in poppy seeds and centre each
daisy with a ball. Bake in a moderate oven (170°C, 350°F) for 12–15
minutes. Allow to cool on baking trays.

Beef and potato curry

Would you believe I cooked my first curry only after leaving Ceylon? Here, for beginners (like I was then), is how to cook a simple curry and the rice that goes with it.

Cut 500 g (1 lb) stewing beef into cubes. Peel and cube 2 large potatoes. Peel and finely chop 2 large onions, 2 large cloves garlic (more if you only have small cloves) and a piece of fresh ginger the size of your first thumb joint (don't look at your thumbs and worry about the size — in this recipe, near enough is good enough!).

In a medium-sized saucepan, preferably one with a heavy base, heat 3 tablespoons oil and fry the chopped onion, garlic and ginger on a medium-low heat, stirring now and then, until the onion becomes first translucent and then starts to turn golden. Add 1 tablespoon good curry powder. Purists don't favour ready-mixed powder, but when you're starting out don't worry about that, just choose a good brand that is packed in a tin, not in a cardboard container. Fry, stirring, for 1 minute. Add a small splash of lemon juice (or about 1 tablespoon vinegar) and fry again until liquid evaporates.

Add 1 teaspoon salt, then put in the meat and fry, stirring, until meat is well coated with the spice mixture and has changed colour. Add about 1 cup peeled, seeded, diced tomato. Very ripe tomatoes are more suitable than expensive, firm salad tomatoes.

Turn heat very low under saucepan, cover with lid and simmer for 45 minutes. Stir every 20 minutes or so to ensure curry doesn't stick to base of pan. If the heat is low enough you won't need to add any water — the juices in the meat will come out, and will then cook down to give a tremendous flavour. Add the potatoes and, if necessary, add about 1 cup water so potatoes are submerged in gravy. Cover and cook a further 20 minutes or until potatoes are done. Serve with hot fluffy rice or rice pilau. Serves 4 or 5.

Rice Pilau: You might as well add some flavour and excitement to the rice (though plain white rice, properly cooked, is delicious with curry). Fry a small onion, finely sliced, in 2 tablespoons each of oil and butter, together with a cinnamon stick and a few cardamom pods (optional). When onion is golden, add 1 teaspoon ground turmeric and stir, then add 500 g (1 lb or $2\frac{1}{2}$ cups) long-grain rice and toss and stir until all the grains are golden. Add 4 cups hot stock or water, 2 teaspoons salt, stir, bring to the boil. Now turn heat as low as it will go, cover saucepan with a well-fitting lid and cook (without lifting lid) exactly 20 minutes. Uncover and let steam escape for a few minutes, then serve with curry and accompaniments such as diced tomatoes and sliced spring onions sprinkled with salt and lemon juice; finely sliced cucumbers in sour cream or yoghurt; sweet chutney, or sliced ripe bananas.

MOMENT OF BIRTH

Again the sweet, life-giving pain
sweeps over me.
Like waves upon a shore,
surging,
receding,
it fades . . . . and then envelops me once more.
And in between its fierceness and its fire
a great and tired peace.
The pulse of life within me
beats triumphantly.

Statistics say
a child is born each moment of the day.
Confronted by this thought,
my consciousness
shrinks.
This wave, this pain, is not just mine alone.
I am no shore . . . .
I am but one of many grains of sand
sharing a common wave.
Multiplied a million times, I become
insignificant.

And yet,
the moment that my child was born
I was no more a tiny grain of sand.
It seemed in all the world
I stood alone.
And God reached down and touched me with His hand.

V
A CHILD IS BORN

Is there any experience more fulfilling than giving birth? If there is, I don't know it. I loved having babies in spite of the built-in discomfort and risks. I don't think I've ever been as "high" as I was after our first child was born. The elation! The joy! The pride! The relief!

She was born around ten o'clock at night and I didn't get to sleep until after four in the morning, spending the hours re-living the experience and talking to my mother who, I guess, was more worn out than I was by the time I finally drifted off. I left the hospital a week later, promising to be back the next year for a repeat performance. I was!

Having babies in Ceylon was quite unlike having babies in Australia. There was always an *ayah* (children's nurse) who lived in and took over the care of the baby completely. All mother had to do was nurse the baby and enjoy it. The realities of washing dozens of nappies and coping with all the other duties never intruded.

In addition, I had mother, father, grandmother and aunties to dote on the child and share the responsibility. No wonder I blithely embarked upon another baby very quickly. This was fun! When the nurse who looked after the toddler offered to mind the new baby as well, I rebuked her, saying no woman could look after two children and do a good job.

Hardly a year later I was eating my words. We had emigrated to Australia, and who do you think had to mind two children *and* run a house and cook and wash and clean? Right. ME! But my husband, bless him, was marvellous, taking over in the kitchen until I got myself sorted out. He had always liked to cook, and I knew I could depend on him to produce a simple yet quite delicious meal.

There is a special kind of food that is appropriate in a home with a new baby in it. Nothing too spicy that might upset the nursing infant, nothing that requires too much preparation time. There will be plenty of opportunities for gourmet cooking later on — now is the time for the new mother to rest and enjoy her baby. Here are Chicken Soup with Rice, and Bread and Butter Pudding, favourites with us when something simple and nourishing is required, and appealing to adults and small children alike.

little Latecomer

Thank you, Lord, for this little one you have blessed me with
so late in life.
I thought I had finished with four-hourly feeds,
nappies,
three-month colic,
immunisations, teething problems—
all those "fringe benefits" that come with babies,
but here I am,
up to my eyes in them.
After eight years, we're starting all over again.

My friends are aghast.
"What about your career?" they say.
But, Lord, I'm not sorry.
Unplanned and unexpected he may have been,
but never for a moment unwanted or unwelcome.

I was scared at first.
"I'm too old," I thought. "What if something goes wrong?"
But oh, the joy of feeling within me
the heaviness of a child growing,
the wonder of all those little — and later, not so little — movements.
The old, yet always new miracle of birth,
the deep welling contentment as he feeds at my breast.

I feel young again, Lord.
What nicer thing could happen to a woman almost forty?
Knowing this is my last child makes me exquisitely aware of every moment.
Thank you for once more letting me be a mother.
I would not have missed it for the world.

Chicken soup with rice

Reuben tells me this is the kind of soup his mother used to make. I don't
know how reliable his memory is, but certainly the soup is very savoury
and practically cooks itself. The children love it. A comforting dish to be
supped with a spoon.

Chop or slice 1 large onion. Heat 2 tablespoons oil or butter in a large
saucepan and cook onion until golden-brown. Add 1 teaspoon turmeric
(a mild spice that gives colour and flavour) and fry, stirring, for a few
seconds. Add a jointed chicken, 1 ripe tomato (chopped), a few sprigs of
celery leaves, 2 cloves garlic (optional), and 2 litres (8 cups) water. Add
2 teaspoons salt or to taste, and bring to the boil. Dribble in 1 cup rice and
cook on low heat, covered, until rice is very soft and chicken spoon-tender,
about 1¼ hours. Taste, adjust seasoning as needed, and serve hot. Serves
4–6. Leftovers taste good, too.

Bread and butter pudding

A simple sweet, good for using up slightly stale bread. Trim crusts off 4 or 5
slices of bread, then butter slices on both sides. The exact number of slices
depends on the size of your pie dish; use a fairly small one for a moister
pudding. Cut each slice in four diagonally. Put a layer of bread in buttered
pie dish and sprinkle with a few sultanas. Repeat with more bread and
sultanas, finishing with a layer of bread.

Beat 2 large eggs with 2 tablespoons sugar and 1 teaspoon vanilla essence.
In a saucepan bring 2 cups milk almost to boiling point and pour over the
beaten eggs, stirring. Pour into the pie dish, allow to stand 30 minutes or
longer, then sprinkle top lightly with sugar, set the dish in a pan of hot
water and bake in a moderate oven (170°C, 350°F) until top is golden-
brown and crusty. Serve warm.

VI
HARD TIMES

One of the best shields against the "slings and arrows of outrageous fortune" is a sense of humour. Potato and beef croquettes are hardly gourmet fare, but I'm sure they tasted all the better when we called them "Croquettes à la Bank Manager" — thanks to whom we were able to buy meat at all. And how does "Paprika Tripe 'In the Red'" grab you? It certainly helped us get through the months when *we* were in the red.

I'm sure I don't have to tell you that money doesn't buy happiness, but it sure helps to have some handy. A spell of bad health, an accident that lays the breadwinner low and makes work impossible for some months, an unexpected pregnancy and loss of a job — we've known all these things, and all at the same time, too. But keeping one's chin up has an advantage: the view is better from that angle!

Paprika tripe "in the red"
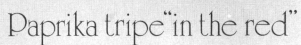

When we were so broke that steak was out of the question we discovered how good tripe can be. It was brought to our attention because Reuben had been in hospital after an accident that threatened his sight, and the hospital served tripe at least twice a week. He grew to like it and, when he came home, asked me to cook it for him. Since then tripe has become fashionable — mostly because people are discovering how good it is cooked the Italian way, simmered in a fruity white wine and sprinkled with grated Parmesan cheese at the table. You can add wine to this recipe, too, instead of water, but I'm giving you the spartan recipe we used and encourage you to improvise and do your own thing.

To serve six people you will need 1 kg (2 lbs) honeycomb tripe, washed, drained and cut into large squares. Set tripe aside and finely chop 3 large onions and 4 cloves garlic (preferably big ones). In a heavy saucepan heat about 3 tablespoons oil and throw in the onions, garlic and a bay leaf. Cook over medium heat, stirring now and then, until the onions are soft and golden, then add 3 or 4 teaspoons paprika, $1\frac{1}{2}$ teaspoons salt and a dash of white pepper. Add the tripe and $1\frac{1}{2}$ cups water (or wine or tomato juice, according to taste and the state of the budget), bring to simmering point, cover and simmer until tripe is tender, about $1\frac{1}{2}$–2 hours. If gravy needs thickening, stir in a little at a time 1 tablespoon plain (all purpose) flour mixed smoothly with 2 teaspoons soft margarine or butter. Serve hot with boiled potatoes or noodles and a green vegetable.

Croquettes à la Bank Manager

It's good going if you can feed six hungry people with half a kilo of meat. I've used a spicy, well-seasoned mince filling because it has to make all that mashed potato taste exciting too. But if you feel that the chillies may provide more excitement than your family is ready for, simply leave them out — the other ingredients will give plenty of flavour. This recipe makes about 18 croquettes.

Finely chop 1 medium onion and 2 cloves garlic. If using them, take 2 fresh green chillies, slit and remove seeds, and chop. Heat 2 tablespoons oil in a medium-sized heavy-based saucepan and gently fry onion, garlic and chillies with ½ teaspoon finely grated fresh ginger until soft. Add 2 teaspoons ground coriander, 1 teaspoon ground cummin and 500 g (1 lb) minced beef. Fry over medium heat, stirring all the time, until the meat changes colour. Add 1½ teaspoons salt and ½ teaspoon ground black pepper, cover and cook over low heat until meat is tender (there should be no liquid left when the meat is cooked). Remove from heat and stir in 2 tablespoons finely chopped fresh mint or coriander leaves (cilantro). Set aside to cool and when completely cold mix through 6 finely chopped spring onions.

Cook 1 kg (2 lbs) potatoes in boiling salted water until tender. Drain well and mash until smooth. Season to taste with salt and pepper. Take roughly 2 tablespoons of mashed potato in one hand, flatten slightly, then place 1 tablespoon of meat mixture in the centre. Mould potato around meat and form into an oval shape. Repeat until all the meat and potato is used up.

Dip croquettes one at a time in an egg that's been lightly beaten, then roll them in dry breadcrumbs. Deep fry in hot oil until golden-brown. Drain on absorbent paper and serve hot with a green vegetable or salad.

Stuffed baked vegetables

A case of tomatoes or a huge bag of sweet peppers at the height of the season is often ridiculously cheap. Try them stuffed and baked as a change from salads. It's also a great way to use up those giant overgrown zucchinis that home gardeners often find lurking under the leaves.

For six people you will need 12 tomatoes, 6 large sweet peppers or 1 large zucchini. Cut tops off tomatoes at the stem end and scoop out the seeds. Following the recipe for Croquettes à la Bank Manager (page 45), make up the minced beef filling. Mix the cooled filling with 1 cup cooked brown rice. Season to taste. Place tomato shells in a greased baking dish. Into each put enough of the meat mixture to completely fill, then scatter some breadcrumbs and a little grated cheese over the top. Dot with margarine or butter and bake in a moderately hot oven (190°C, 375°F) for 20–30 minutes, or until tomatoes are soft and cooked.

    If you are using peppers, cut off the stem ends, then scoop out and discard seeds. Parboil for 5 minutes, then drain and fill as for tomatoes. With zucchini, cut in half lengthways, scoop out and discard seeds. Parboil for 5 minutes or until softened but still holding its shape. Drain, and proceed as for tomatoes.

Macaroni cheese

Use a large shallow baking dish rather than a deep casserole for this recipe, and you'll get more of the toasted crust which everyone wants. As an extra saving use skim milk powder for making the milk sauce, but do put in a good amount of cheese.

To serve six people take 375 g (12 oz) elbow macaroni (or any suitable pasta) and cook in plenty of boiling salted water until just tender. Drain in a colander. Melt 90 g (3 oz) margarine or butter in a saucepan and stir in $\frac{1}{2}$ cup plain (all purpose) flour and stir over low heat for 1 minute to cook the flour. Take pan off the heat and briskly stir in 3 cups milk. Bring to the boil, stirring all the time, and simmer 2–3 minutes.

Grate 250 g (8 oz) natural Cheddar cheese and stir all but $\frac{1}{2}$ cup into the sauce. Add drained macaroni and pile into a greased shallow baking dish. Mix $\frac{1}{2}$ cup dry breadcrumbs with remaining cheese and scatter over the top. Dot with margarine and bake in a moderately hot oven (190°C, 375°F) for 20 minutes or until golden and crusty on top.

WHEN BAD THINGS HAPPEN

Lord,
I can't help wondering why
you let this happen.
In my bewilderment and pain I asked,
"Lord, what are you doing to me?"
Clearly came the answer,
"Giving you a chance to show you really trust me."

Like a sudden ray of light
it searched out a truth I had quite overlooked.
I've sung my songs and praised you
when the path ahead was bright,
but now you're asking me to step into the darkness
with only your word to stand upon.

Only your word? Forgive me, Lord.
For your word is sure.
Men write contracts, witness and sign them,
then find a loophole to render them null and void.
But you give us your word, and your word is yourself.
You are the same yesterday,
today, forever.

So Lord, let me not miss the chance
to trust you.
To love you who first loved me.
To walk by faith when I cannot see.

Let me, dear Lord, sing my sweetest song
in the night.

Give Me A Holiday Heart

Lord, the little face is so eager,
so glowing with excitement,
so lit with smiles.
"Clap hands, clap hands!
We are going to the Snowies tomorrow."

Forgive me my lack of joy,
forgive the grudging consent
to this holiday in the snow.
But, you see, I've done it all before
so many times, and I know
that four children in a caravan
are not exactly what the doctor ordered
for rest and relaxation.
Already I regard the running hot water
with the fondness reserved for a dear friend,
and involuntarily I shiver
at the thought of the cold.

Lord, I'm sorry, but I completely lack the pioneer spirit.
I love the comforts of my home
and cannot understand why
a pipe and slippers type like you-know-who
should suffer this annual madness
and head towards the mountains
with caravan in tow
and argumentative kids in the back seat.

This time, Lord,
help me to really enter into the spirit of the thing.
Help me to be truly glad that we can make this trip
Help me to be thankful for the chance
of having the family all together.
Soon they'll be grown and these holidays
will be a thing of the past.

Lord, help me to be as joyful as the littlest one,
hardly able to wait for his first glimpse of snow,
planning to make a snowman
(and even, he confided, hoping to drop in on Santa —
in his mind a natural association).

I must go now — there's still so much to do,
and we must make an early start tomorrow.
Be with us, Lord, take us in health and safety,
bring us back refreshed,
and may we all — especially me — enjoy your wonderful world.

55

VII

HOLIDAYS
ON A SHOESTRING

How do you feel about holidays? I know that as the time draws near I get the feeling that if I can hold out these few weeks longer I might just make it and survive another year. The tiredness builds up and the thought of a break is like an oasis in the desert.

But there is the other side of things. On some holidays mum and dad work very hard. Especially when the children are young, it seems almost too much to pack the numerous changes of clothing and dozens of nappies.

Husband, bless him, is a great enthusiast for holidays on the move. So we'd hire a caravan and take the children away, sometimes by the sea, sometimes to the snow. When they were little they gave us some bad moments. A sudden stomach pain in the middle of the night, miles from anywhere. Could it be appendicitis? And the hunt for suitable toilet facilities in pouring rain. Notice how it always seems to rain during such holidays?

As the children grew up and became more independent, there wasn't quite so much to do for them, and indeed they helped. But oh, how they could argue. In the confines of a caravan or a car, the mixture of personalities kept in close contact was nothing short of explosive! But we've had so much fun, and, if nothing else, the children will have some memories to chuckle over.

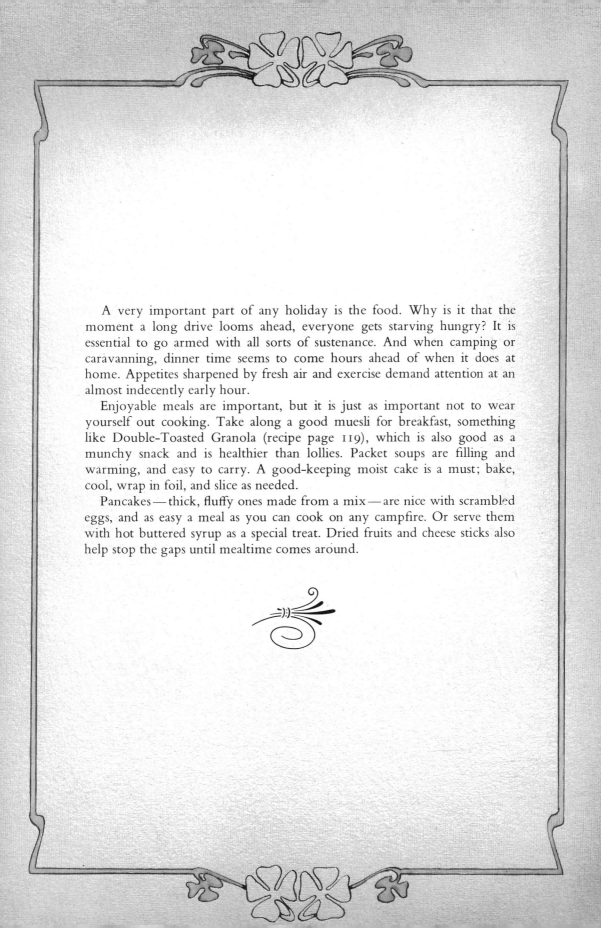

A very important part of any holiday is the food. Why is it that the moment a long drive looms ahead, everyone gets starving hungry? It is essential to go armed with all sorts of sustenance. And when camping or caravanning, dinner time seems to come hours ahead of when it does at home. Appetites sharpened by fresh air and exercise demand attention at an almost indecently early hour.

Enjoyable meals are important, but it is just as important not to wear yourself out cooking. Take along a good muesli for breakfast, something like Double-Toasted Granola (recipe page 119), which is also good as a munchy snack and is healthier than lollies. Packet soups are filling and warming, and easy to carry. A good-keeping moist cake is a must; bake, cool, wrap in foil, and slice as needed.

Pancakes — thick, fluffy ones made from a mix — are nice with scrambled eggs, and as easy a meal as you can cook on any campfire. Or serve them with hot buttered syrup as a special treat. Dried fruits and cheese sticks also help stop the gaps until mealtime comes around.

Corned beef hash

This recipe calls for a can of corned beef and cold cooked potato left over from a previous meal. Slice 3 onions and cook in a little oil or butter until good and brown. This is important for flavour. Slice cold cooked potatoes and add to pan with diced corned beef. Fry until potatoes are golden. Season with Worcestershire sauce and tomato or chilli sauce if liked. Heat through and serve.

Barbecue marinade

The best part of those camping or caravanning trips or even just a day's outing is the barbecue meal in the open air. Here is a marinade to take with you in a screw-top jar. Meat bought fresh from a country butcher responds well to a short soaking in some of this *teriyaki*-style marinade.

Crush 1 small clove garlic with 1 teaspoon sugar and put into a screw-top jar with ½ teaspoon finely grated fresh ginger, 6 tablespoons each of soy sauce and dry sherry, and, if liked, 1 teaspoon oriental sesame oil. Shake well before use.

Carrot cake

A marvellous tasting, good-keeping loaf. Brush a fairly large loaf tin with oil. Line base with greaseproof paper and brush paper with oil. Preheat oven to moderate (170°C, 350°F).

Put into a mixing bowl ¾ cup each of raw sugar and corn oil *or* sunflower oil. Add 2 teaspoons vanilla essence, give a few quick stirs. Add 3 large eggs one at a time and beat well after each is added. Sift together twice 2 cups plain wholemeal flour, 4½ teaspoons baking powder, 1 teaspoon cake spice or grated nutmeg, and ½ teaspoon salt. Stir into oil and egg mixture. Coarsely grate enough carrots to yield 1½ cups and add to mixture together with ½ cup finely chopped almonds, walnuts or sunflower seeds.

Turn into prepared tin and bake in a moderate oven for 1¼ hours or until a skewer thrust into the centre comes out clean. If the top browns too quickly, cover with a piece of brown paper or foil. Cool cake in tin for 10 minutes, then turn out onto a wire rack. It is nice warm or cold, and improves in flavour if cooled completely and wrapped in foil for a day before being served either plain or buttered.

VIII
FRIENDSHIP
IS SHARING A RECIPE

Maggie's home~made French mustard

Maggie is a girl who enjoys cooking and loves food with a sheer sensuous delight that is a joy to behold. Her enthusiasm is infectious, and I love cooking and working with her. She it was who goaded me into organising this book, girded me with encouragement and praise, and guarded me from interruptions until, at last, the manuscript was done. To Maggie, sounding board and typiste extraordinaire, my undying thanks.

Place 2 cups whole yellow mustard seed in a glass bowl with 2–3 whole dried chillies and a bay leaf. Add enough white wine vinegar to cover, then put a plate on top and set aside overnight.

Next day, remove chillies and bay leaf. A little at a time, blend half the soaked seeds in an electric blender, adding enough dry white wine to keep the mixture free moving. Mix blended mustard with remaining soaked mustard seeds and sweeten to taste with honey (a good 2–3 tablespoons). Add more white wine if necessary for soft, moist consistency.

Spoon into glass jars, push a dried chilli or two into each jar, and seal with lids. Make sure the lids are plastic-lined or they will be eaten by the acid. Put in a dark cupboard to mature for at least three months, though a year is better. Make it up early in the year for next Christmas's gifts.

Beryl's hot cheese snack

Beryl is one of the truly beautiful people. What would I have done without her comfort and support in the early days when she befriended this timid migrant? She has a heart that is open to every need. She is convinced she is no cook, but that is unbelievable for someone who has reared three healthy boys to manhood. When I told her I needed a recipe to represent her in this chapter she said, "You're kidding." I'm sure she creates dishes all the time, but is just not aware of it. Her contribution is something very simple, but just the thing for a family of always hungry boys. Quick to make for breakfast, lunch or a light Sunday supper.

Arrange on heated plates rashers of grilled bacon and slices of tomato. Keep warm while dipping thick slices of natural mild cheese in beaten egg, then in breadcrumbs, and frying quickly in hot oil. Cook to a golden colour on both sides, drain briefly on the frying spoon or a food slice, place on tomatoes and serve at once.

Jill's Irish Cream pie

Jill is a superb cook, a country woman whose kitchen and garden and entire house shine with her talents. She makes the best brined olives I have tasted, a process that requires much time and patience. She also makes a great Irish Cream Pie, and was delighted to pass on the recipe.

Make and bake the pastry first. For this beat together 1 egg and ½ cup caster sugar until lemon-coloured, then add 185 g (6 oz) soft butter or margarine and a squeeze of lemon juice (the lemon juice is not essential but it seems to help the handling of the pastry in hot weather). Sift together 2½ cups plain (all purpose) flour and 1 teaspoon baking powder and fold into creamed mixture only enough to combine ingredients, particularly if the weather is warm. In summer, chill pastry well before using but in winter it can be used straight away. Never over-handle the pastry because of its high fat content. In hot weather it is easier to roll it between two sheets of plastic wrap or waxed paper. Sufficient for two 22.5 cm (9 inch) pie shells.

   Place pastry in lightly greased pie plates, prick well. (Jill says this is a very well-behaved pastry and doesn't need weighting down for cooking). Bake in a moderate oven (170°C, 350°F) for 12–15 minutes until lightly golden. Cool. (Freeze one, then the next pie is made in half the time.)

   While the case is cooling make the filling. Sprinkle 2½ teaspoons gelatine over 3 tablespoons hot water in a cup. Stir to dissolve, then leave to cool. Beat 125 g (4 oz) cream cheese until smooth, add 1 tablespoon honey and 1 tablespoon sugar and beat until light. Separate 2 eggs and add yolks one at a time to creamed mixture, beating well after each is added. Mix in dissolved gelatine and ½ cup Irish Cream liqueur. Beat well. Whip a generous ½ cup cream until it holds in soft peaks, then fold into mixture. Beat egg whites until stiff, then fold through. Pour into cooled pastry case and chill in refrigerator.

   Pipe a decorative edge around pie with **Coffee Cream:** Dissolve 2 teaspoons sugar and 1 teaspoon coffee granules in 1 tablespoon water. Mix in ½ teaspoon cinnamon powder. Pour into a bowl with ½ cup cream and whip until it forms peaks, then pipe onto pie edge. Just before serving, decorate with 30 g (1 oz) chocolate shaved into curls with a vegetable peeler. Serves 8–10.

LETTER TO A FRIEND

This is just to say "I love you",
words so seldom spoken save by lovers
or to children very young.
Yet they are so fit to tell our friends
of what is in our hearts. People shrink
from sounding soft. Could they but realise
that love's the noblest feeling that we have
for one another, so there is no shame
in saying it aloud. How shy we are
to let our thoughts, conceived in mind and heart,
have form and birth through words. So many thoughts
of kindliness and love are never known
because we hesitate to use this gift,
this priceless gift of words. I use them now
to tell you that I thank the Lord of life,
among all things, for such a friend as you.
Across the differences of race and creed,
across my fears and loneliness and need,
your friendship reaches out. I'm not alone.
This is no trifling thing, but treasure rare.
And though we may not often meet and talk,
it's wonderful to know that you are there.

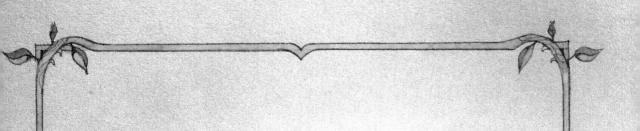

Val's coffee liqueur cream

My friendship with Valerie goes back to our teen years. We laughed and cried together, swapped clothes and confidences, double-dated, made fudge and ice cream which we ate with abandon, and had the usual girlish rows but defended each other fiercely against all criticism. She is the sister I never had, and I love her dearly. But trying to get a recipe from her is sheer hard work. She cooks instinctively, never writes down what she does and is gloriously vague about quantities. So this recipe represents not only Valerie's culinary talents, but also my prowess as a detective!

Sprinkle $1\frac{1}{2}$ tablespoons unflavoured gelatine over $\frac{1}{3}$ cup of cold water and leave 5 minutes to swell and soften. In $1\frac{1}{2}$ cups hot water dissolve 1 tablespoon instant coffee granules. Empty the contents of one 410 g (14 oz) can sweetened condensed milk into a bowl, add hot coffee to can and stir well to dissolve milk remaining in can. Add to condensed milk and stir.

Stand cup containing softened gelatine in a small saucepan of simmering water until gelatine dissolves. Stir into coffee and milk. Add $\frac{1}{4}$ cup Tia Maria or other coffee liqueur and, if liked, $\frac{1}{4}$ cup cream. Mix well and pour into a glass dessert dish or individual small dessert dishes. Refrigerate until firm and well chilled. Serves 6–8.

The Visit

I dropped in and you weren't home,
but I lingered a while in your garden
and it was as if we met.

For you were there in the delicate bloom of the wisteria,
the clump of violets under the apple tree,
the jasmine and the red rose climbing together, intertwined,
the frilly, pink and white azalea.
Best of all, the orange tree laden with waxy blossom,
windblown petals scattered like snow beneath the branches,
wearing an aura of perfume and busy, honey-seeking bees.

I'll be back to speak to you tomorrow,
but it was nice seeing you today.

IX
HAND~ME~DOWNS

I grew up surrounded by good cooks — two generations of them.
My father's mother I remember as a stately lady with abundant
silver hair piled on top of her head. I was only six years old when
she died, but her recipes lived on. At least eleven years after her
death we were still opening (and enjoying) jars of the wine-red, sparkling
clear fruit jellies she had made; and her daughters long continued her proud
tradition of winning gold and silver medals at exhibitions.

Nowhere else have I seen anything prepared with the sort of meticulous
care that my aunts lavished on their cooking. From time to time they made
small batches of very special chutneys and pickles. The whole kitchen would
be cleared and given over to sterilising bottles, peeling and chopping and
coring and slicing; then the cooking, and the bottling, and finally sealing in
the precious results with corks and shiny, dark-red sealing wax. I remember
a tale, proudly told in the family, that when dignitaries from our island (then
part of the British Empire) visited England, they took gifts for the British
royal family — not only silver and the valuable gems for which Ceylon (or
Sri Lanka, as it's now called, though I always remember it as Ceylon) is still
famous, but also bottles of the island's best condiments. Ours! My aunts
used to speculate on the likelihood of our chutneys ending up on a table in
Buckingham Palace.

Some of these magnificent condiments were offered for sale in the small,
exclusive shop that was my aunts' occupation and preoccupation. It was not,
I suspect, a business they depended upon financially, for it was a wonderful
olde worlde type of establishment where the people who came through the
doors were not there just for a quick business transaction but for conversation
and the exchange of the day's news in the best tradition of a small town.

My aunts sold ribbons and fine laces and buttons, greeting cards and
novelties, and the most wonderful imported chocolates and sweets and
biscuits. Even now I recall visiting them, as a child of five or six, and being
allowed to choose a favourite sweet. I remember too that most often I reached
into a particular tall glass jar among other tall glass jars, the one that held
dark chocolate discs individually wrapped in silver paper. How I delighted
in pressing down with my thumb on the depression in the centre so that the
paper went "pop" around the edge!

I was given my grandmother's brass preserving pan when my aunts were too old to carry on cooking, and it now hangs, gleaming softly, on my kitchen wall except when I take it down to make a batch of jam or jelly. I get so much pleasure from using this pan. It is not my imagination — it *does* make better jam and jelly than any of the newer pans I used before I came into possession of this treasure.

Another heirloom was given to me by Aunt Millie and stands proudly in a place of honour in our living room, too beautiful to be put away in a kitchen cupboard. It is a heavy brass mortar and pestle, so well used and lovingly cared for over many generations that it shines like gold. I shall never forget how touched I was when Aunt Millie, who was then over eighty, frail and blind, said to me, "This belonged to my grandmother, and I want you to have it." A gift of diamonds could not have pleased me more. I use it (it would be a shame not to), but only for very special, fragrant ingredients like cinnamon and cardamom and the world's most expensive spice, saffron. I recall Aunt Millie using it for spices too.

Then there is the decorative mould of sparkling, heatproof glass in which I bake *breudher* each Christmas and New Year. This was given to me by my father's youngest and only surviving sister, Aunt Claribel. There was this mould and another larger one, identical in shape. I could sense, as she gave them to me, that though she wanted me to use them, it was the end of an era. It was as if she were severing a link with her sister, my Aunt Elva, who had recently died and whose pride and joy these moulds had been.

We packed them with the greatest care, putting layers of cloth between the larger mould and the smaller one, then surrounding them with more packing. In spite of all our precautions, the air journey proved too much. When I unpacked the parcel I found that the larger mould was broken. I decided not to tell Aunt Clarie, but she kept writing, asking whether they had survived the journey.

I told her, quite truthfully, that I had baked a *breudher* in the glass pan. She was astute enough to realise I had referred to them in the singular. Again she questioned and I could not lie, so the awful truth was told. If only she knew how well the remaining mould is cared for, how joyfully it is used, and how much it is admired.

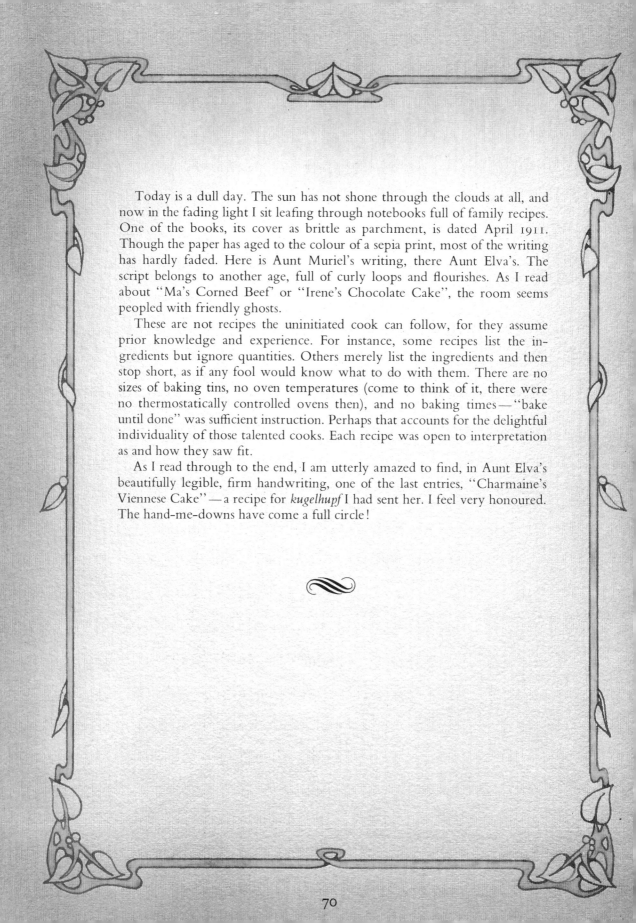

Today is a dull day. The sun has not shone through the clouds at all, and now in the fading light I sit leafing through notebooks full of family recipes. One of the books, its cover as brittle as parchment, is dated April 1911. Though the paper has aged to the colour of a sepia print, most of the writing has hardly faded. Here is Aunt Muriel's writing, there Aunt Elva's. The script belongs to another age, full of curly loops and flourishes. As I read about "Ma's Corned Beef" or "Irene's Chocolate Cake", the room seems peopled with friendly ghosts.

These are not recipes the uninitiated cook can follow, for they assume prior knowledge and experience. For instance, some recipes list the ingredients but ignore quantities. Others merely list the ingredients and then stop short, as if any fool would know what to do with them. There are no sizes of baking tins, no oven temperatures (come to think of it, there were no thermostatically controlled ovens then), and no baking times — "bake until done" was sufficient instruction. Perhaps that accounts for the delightful individuality of those talented cooks. Each recipe was open to interpretation as and how they saw fit.

As I read through to the end, I am utterly amazed to find, in Aunt Elva's beautifully legible, firm handwriting, one of the last entries, "Charmaine's Viennese Cake" — a recipe for *kugelhupf* I had sent her. I feel very honoured. The hand-me-downs have come a full circle!

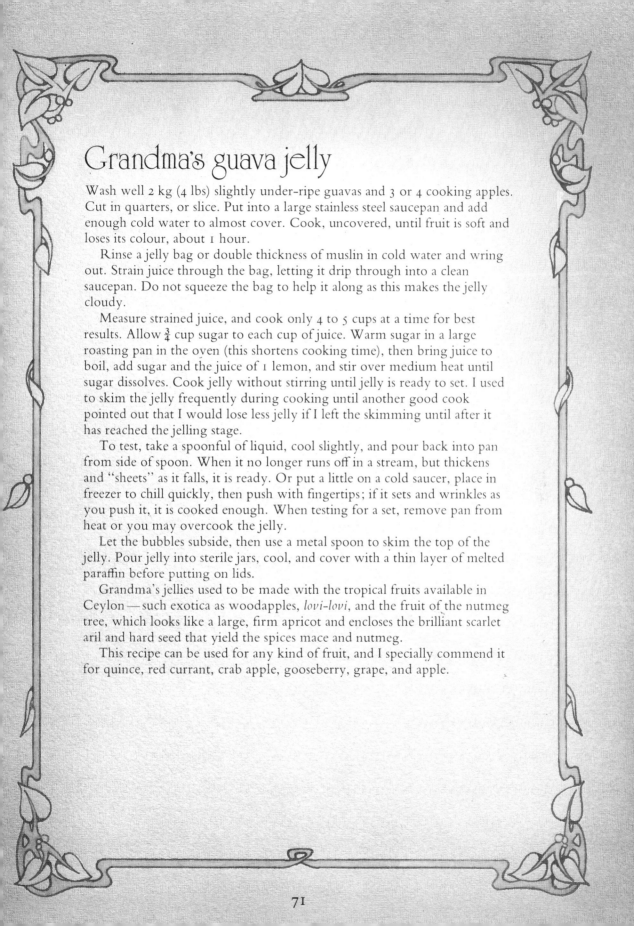

Grandma's guava jelly

Wash well 2 kg (4 lbs) slightly under-ripe guavas and 3 or 4 cooking apples.
Cut in quarters, or slice. Put into a large stainless steel saucepan and add
enough cold water to almost cover. Cook, uncovered, until fruit is soft and
loses its colour, about 1 hour.

Rinse a jelly bag or double thickness of muslin in cold water and wring
out. Strain juice through the bag, letting it drip through into a clean
saucepan. Do not squeeze the bag to help it along as this makes the jelly
cloudy.

Measure strained juice, and cook only 4 to 5 cups at a time for best
results. Allow $\frac{3}{4}$ cup sugar to each cup of juice. Warm sugar in a large
roasting pan in the oven (this shortens cooking time), then bring juice to
boil, add sugar and the juice of 1 lemon, and stir over medium heat until
sugar dissolves. Cook jelly without stirring until jelly is ready to set. I used
to skim the jelly frequently during cooking until another good cook
pointed out that I would lose less jelly if I left the skimming until after it
has reached the jelling stage.

To test, take a spoonful of liquid, cool slightly, and pour back into pan
from side of spoon. When it no longer runs off in a stream, but thickens
and "sheets" as it falls, it is ready. Or put a little on a cold saucer, place in
freezer to chill quickly, then push with fingertips; if it sets and wrinkles as
you push it, it is cooked enough. When testing for a set, remove pan from
heat or you may overcook the jelly.

Let the bubbles subside, then use a metal spoon to skim the top of the
jelly. Pour jelly into sterile jars, cool, and cover with a thin layer of melted
paraffin before putting on lids.

Grandma's jellies used to be made with the tropical fruits available in
Ceylon — such exotica as woodapples, *lovi-lovi*, and the fruit of the nutmeg
tree, which looks like a large, firm apricot and encloses the brilliant scarlet
aril and hard seed that yield the spices mace and nutmeg.

This recipe can be used for any kind of fruit, and I specially commend it
for quince, red currant, crab apple, gooseberry, grape, and apple.

Time out for Dreaming

I once came across a lovely old recipe for rose petal conserve. It was written in quaint seventeenth-century English, but was simple enough, and I knew I just had to try it.

It was summer, and in my garden
red roses bloomed with ridiculous abandon;
even leaving all the buds (I couldn't bear to pick them),
there was a big basket full.

Reading the recipe,
sorting and choosing the best petals,
simmering and stirring
with the fragrance of roses around me,
I was dressed in sprigged muslin
and starched white cap,
in another time, another place.

When I had done, there were just a few tiny jars.
A waste of time?
But then, I wasn't only making conserve,
I was making a memory.

X
CHILDHOOD DAYS

There have been many jokes on the theme "Are you a housewife or do you work?", and they aren't funny to the homemaker who has been on the go from dawn to dark and then wakes up in the middle of the night to care for a sick child or soothe one who is afraid.

Having experienced stay-at-home periods as well as going to an office, I know that one is just as busy, and more constantly on call, when at home. But there are compensations — sweet compensations not to be equalled by a job promotion or a substantial increase in salary.

I recall taking my small son for a walk, equipped with paper and poster colours. He was going to paint a picture of the autumn colours of the trees in the next street. As he trotted beside me, chubby hand in mine, the angelic face beamed and he said, "Isn't it a beautiful day, Mummy? Only God can shine up a day like this."

Once, when he was recovering from an illness, I made soap bubble mixture and rolled some pipes from paper and we blew bubbles, sitting on the swing in the back garden, and watched them take on rainbow colours before they grew heavy and plopped into nothingness.

I wish I could remember more. So many lovely moments have vanished from memory. Before you know it, children grow up.

If you spend as much time in the kitchen as most mothers do, it is a good idea to give youngsters a keen interest in what goes on there. I've found the kitchen has an irresistible attraction, and even pre-schoolers can produce quite edible offerings with a little encouragement.

I bought a small rolling pin and encouraged the rolling out of pastry and cookies. Most children love doing this. And when they come to that independent stage when they don't want mother to help at all, there are some recipes that require only mixing and shaping into balls, quite within the scope of tiny hands. These times in the kitchen are to be treasured — there are so many things to talk about, and it won't be long before they're off to school and then this particular delight won't be practical except at weekends or during school holidays.

Here are some recipes my children have enjoyed. Stand by to assist according to age and ability, and be very patient even if they do make a mess — the apprentice will be a great help in a few years' time.

Coconut kisses

Set oven at moderately slow (160 C, 325 F). Line two baking trays with foil and lightly butter the foil.

In a bowl combine 2 cups desiccated coconut, half of a 410 g (14 oz) can sweetened condensed milk, $\frac{1}{2}$ teaspoon vanilla essence and $\frac{1}{4}$ teaspoon almond essence. Mix well with a wooden spoon. Drop teaspoonfuls of mixture on trays or form into tiny peaked shapes by hand. Bake for 8–10 minutes or until touched golden-brown on the peaks. Makes about 30 pieces.

Oil cookies

No creaming or beating with these simple cookies. They are very crisp and will stay that way for days — if they last. The quantity makes about 60 cookies.

Set oven at moderately hot (190 C, 375 F). Line baking trays with foil and grease lightly.

Put 1 cup sugar and $\frac{3}{4}$ cup oil into a bowl and mix together with a wooden spoon. Add 1 teaspoon vanilla essence and 1 egg and mix well. Add 1 more egg and mix again. Sift in 1 cup self-raising flour, $1\frac{1}{2}$ cups plain (all purpose) flour and $\frac{1}{2}$ teaspoon salt, and stir until all the flour is mixed in. If using all plain flour, add 1 teaspoon baking powder.

Take small teaspoons of the dough and roll between palms to form balls. When all the balls are made roll them in some extra sugar, flatten between palms and place on baking trays. Leave a little space between balls as they will spread slightly during baking. Bake for 10 minutes or until golden-brown, remove from oven and allow to cool slightly on tray before lifting them onto a wire rack to finish cooling.

Pikelets

Using a rotary beater mix together 1 large or 2 small eggs, $\frac{3}{4}$ cup milk, a dash of vanilla essence, 2 tablespoons melted butter and 1 tablespoon sugar. Measure 1 cup self-raising flour and a pinch of salt and sift over the top. Beat until batter is thick and smooth.

Heat a frying pan and lightly grease the base. Put spoonfuls of batter into pan, and cook until bubbles form on the surface, then flip over and cook other side. Wrap cooked pikelets in a tea towel to keep warm. Eat them with butter and jam or honey.

It's nine o'clock on a hot summer morning.
Boy stands by the window
looking puzzled,
listening hard.
"I can hear stars!"
"Hear stars?"
"Yes, hear stars."
"You did say 'stars', didn't you?"
"Yes. *Stars*!"
This was beginning to sound
like a nonsense conversation.
"What do you mean, 'hear stars'?"
"You know how you can hear stars at night,
well, I can hear them now."
"I've never heard stars. Do you mean *you* can hear them?"
"Yes, Mummy. Come here and listen."
I went to the window and on the still air
came the sound of insects, an intermittent buzzing.
"All I can hear are cicadas," I said.
"No, cicadas make a different noise."
"Oh well, crickets then. That's all *I* can hear."
A disappointed voice said,
"Oh. I always thought it was
the stars that made that zzzz zzzz zzzz zzzz noise."

I felt almost mean.
Should I have told the truth
and taken the sound of stars from his wonderful world?

THE SOUND OF STARS ❋

Redecorating

"No, no," my heart protests, "not yet.
It's too soon, too soon."
But my eyes tell me it's time.
The bright nursery murals
are tattered now,
the pink and purple hippo sadly faded,
the smiling tiger with the googly eyes
is peeling at the edges,
the gentle jumbo scribbled on.
Only the stylised tree stands tall and straight,
happy owls in its branches eyeing each other lovingly,
their feathers still bright and beautiful.
Even the jolly giraffe, against whom
many matched their quickly changing heights,
looks slightly tired.

How old was he when we did this room? Three? Four?
I can't remember quite.
But I do recall how fiercely independent he was
as he helped me stick the decals
on the freshly painted walls.
"No, *I* do it!" The little arms
too short to reach the designated spot,
yet determination loomed large
and so we got it done,
painstakingly rubbing out the air bubbles,
standing back to admire our private zoo
that had not just animals and birds
but grass and flowers and butterflies too,
and a bright orange sun beaming down. At first
the sun's face didn't wear a smile
and we decided that wouldn't do,
so we painted it on and that made it perfect.

I've always loved this room.
Even the curtains look happy,
with smiling children and balloons.

What will we do with it next?
Fabric with vintage cars?
Posters of space stations and rockets?
At least it isn't due for pin-up girls. Not yet.

No, I won't redecorate right now.
I'll scrub the scribbled-on jumbo,
stick back the tiger's smile
and put off the change that has to come
. . . . . for just a little while.

XI

BIRTHDAYS

As someone wise and witty has already said, "Birthdays are wonderful things for other people to have."

And indeed, from the youthful years when every birthday was a reason to have a party and a new dress and feasting and dancing into the early hours, it has now simmered down to a quiet thankfulness for each year that passes, with all it has brought of joy and sadness, excitement and plodding times.

On my birthday, wherever I am, I send my mother a big bunch of flowers. After all, as I realised when I became a mother myself, it was her valiant effort that is marked by the day—I was merely a passenger.

I love celebrating children's birthdays. They are so special, for them and for me. I remember the first years and those joyous gatherings with parents, aunts and grandparents celebrating my elder daughter's first and second birthdays. Then we immigrated to Australia and my younger daughter had her first birthday far away from fond relatives. Still, we gathered good friends around and I made a birthday cake and created tempting savouries. We have photographs of the tot, unsteady on her feet, attempting to blow out the solitary candle.

Since we had only been in Australia for two months and were still living in a flat, we had not met families with children and the guests were mainly adults. But six months later we had moved into our suburban home, made friends with neighbours, and had a noisy and altogether eye-opening third birthday.

Eye-opening for me, that is. For a week or more before the date I had stayed up night after night making confectionery. Every marshmallow, fondant, marzipan and piece of coconut ice was lovingly home made. Not to mention the dainty "crinoline lady" birthday cake. And what did I find? The children couldn't have cared less whether the sweets were home made or bought at the supermarket. They dived into cocktail franks and potato chips and filled themselves with sandwiches and ice cream and cake, and made lots of noise and enjoyed themselves enormously.

The birthday cake is probably the most important item on the menu. Though it will soon be cut into and demolished, it should be something special. It's all very well for those who have learned cake decorating to turn out works of art. But for those who, like me, have not been fortunate enough and have only limited time, here are some ideas I've used through the years.

Maypole Cake: A simple round cake with a ribbon-wrapped pole in the centre, and ribbons coming from a rosette on the top of the pole to each of the "dancers". Dancers are easily made from cup cakes turned upside down and covered with soft butter icing piped in frills, and with a tiny plastic doll inserted in the top; the cakes form the "skirts".

Ballet Cake: This was when the girls' ballet phase was on. A large slab of chocolate cake is the stage, while Christmas-tree lights wrapped around the sides are lit up as footlights. Ballet dancers are tiny dolls sold cheaply at chain stores and dressed in tutus of tightly gathered tulle. If the dolls are small enough, you don't need to worry about the tops, the tutu covers all!

Crinoline Lady: Bake a cake in a pudding bowl or a special Dolly Varden mould, and top with a small doll (the doll's legs can be pressed into the cake so she is only seen from the waist up). Cover the cake with soft icing or plastic icing to simulate folds of crinoline, and decorate with icing flowers which can be bought ready made.

Musical Cake: When our ten-year-old formed a musical group at school and the "band" was coming over for a rehearsal and birthday celebration combined, it obviously had to be a musical cake. One of the easiest to decorate, it is frosted smoothly in plain butter icing with staves and notes written on in melted chocolate. Pipe the chocolate out of a cone of greaseproof paper, or from a small plastic bag with one corner snipped to make a hole that will let through only a thin line of chocolate.

Treasure Chest Cake: This is ideal for the age when they want to be pirates. Bake a large loaf-shaped cake, and slice off the top third to form a "lid"; cover both pieces of the cake with chocolate icing. The lid is propped open to disclose treasure of gold-covered chocolate coins, brightly coloured gumdrop jewels and other sorts of sweet loot.

Flower Cake: An elegant cake for adult birthdays. The base can be any kind of cake — I favour the rich, nutty tortes layered with smooth butter-cream filling (recipe page 137). The cake, after frosting, looks delicately pretty with sprigs of violets and snowdrops or miniature roses. We decorated a wedding cake with spring blossom, tulle and ribbon, and it looked as pretty as if professionally iced, though naturally it didn't last more than a day. (To crystallise violets, brush the flowers with slightly beaten egg white, sprinkle with caster sugar, and dry on a wire rack.)

BIRTHDAYS

I referred to him as "nine years old",
and he said, "Not nine, Mum. Ten."
"Goodness, are you? Why so you are.
In three months' time it's your birthday again."

Oh God, where have the years gone?
It seems the last time I looked he was five.
It was his birthday.
Someone had given us a dog that needed a home —
a beautiful golden beast much bigger than the boy,
and somehow, right from the start, it was *his* dog.
We churned ice cream on the patio, a special treat.
And of course there was a birthday cake with candles.
Now, all of a sudden, he's ten.
Where did those years go, and when?

I don't know where, but I do know how . . . .
in hurry and rush.
Taking too little time to watch him grow.
"Wake up, you're late, it's time for school."
"Go wash your hands—with *soap*."
"Finish your dinner."
"Are your lessons done?"
With too much work, too little fun,
the years have sped right by.

If I think back I can recall
the year his dad took him and some friends
to the zoo. A new baby was coming,
and it was all I could do
to pack a lunch and stay thankfully at home.
Another birthday we took him and four other noisy boys
on a picnic. That was fun.
And once we had a ride on a train.
A real treat.

There was the year he had a teacher he loved.
She was pretty and kind, and he did so well.
Then there was the year he didn't like his teacher
and his marks fell. And fell.
But these are only small things to remember.
All the while he's been growing, growing.
He's halfway to being a man and I hadn't even realised
my son is almost ten.

Dear God,
whatever else I have,
I can never have those years again.

Birthday cake

For the sake of immature digestive systems, it is wise to use either plain sponges or a light butter cake as the foundation — children turn away from spicy or fruity or too-rich cakes. A little colour never goes amiss, though, and I often make the cake in layers of pink, white and chocolate, or else marble the colours through the mixture. The following recipe is my favourite. It's a light butter cake that keeps fresh for a few days, so if you want to take time to be creative and decorate the cake you can do so a day or two before and not end up with a cake gone dry.

Set oven at moderate (170°C, 350°F). Grease a deep round cake tin 20 to 22.5 cm (8 to 9 inches) in diameter, line base with greased greaseproof paper, and dust tin with flour (tip out any excess flour). If you are making a three-layer rainbow cake, grease and flour three 20 cm (8 inch) sandwich pans. For a Treasure Chest Cake, grease a $25 \times 12.5 \times 10$ cm ($10 \times 5 \times 4$ inches) loaf tin and line base with greased greaseproof paper.

Sift $2\frac{2}{3}$ cups plain (all purpose) flour, then sift again with $2\frac{1}{4}$ teaspoons baking powder and $\frac{1}{2}$ teaspoon salt. Cream 250 g (8 oz) butter until soft, then add 2 cups sugar very gradually, beating until light. Separate 4 eggs and add yolks one at a time, beating well after each is added. Mix in 2 teaspoons vanilla essence. Measure out 1 cup milk and add to creamed mixture in thirds alternately with the sifted flour mixture. Beat egg whites until stiff, then fold in gently.

Turn into prepared cake tin and bake 1 hour in moderate oven. The cake will need to be covered with brown paper or foil for the last 15 minutes of cooking. Test with a fine skewer in centre of cake and, when it comes out clean, remove cake from oven and allow to cool completely on a wire rack before decorating.

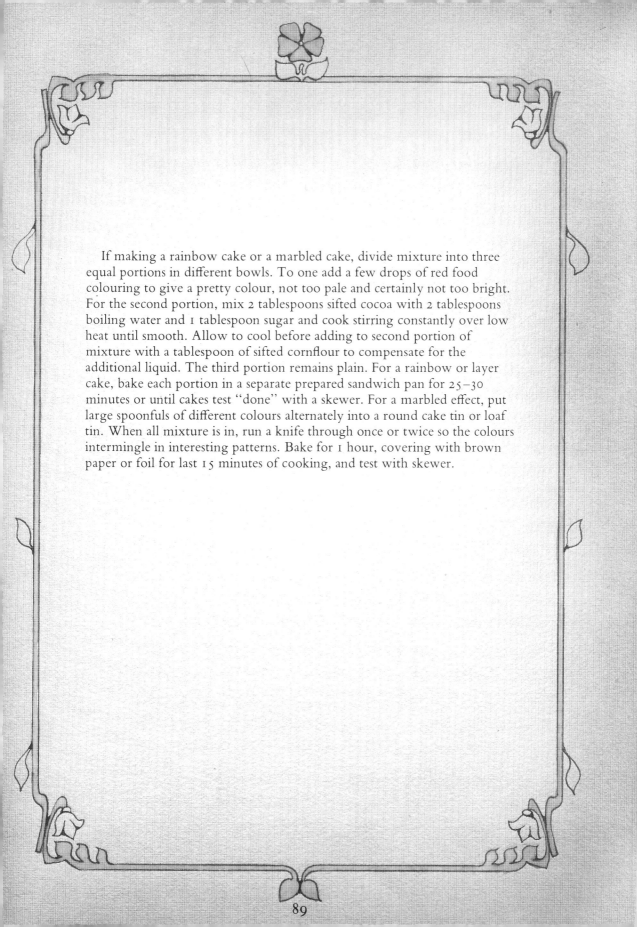

If making a rainbow cake or a marbled cake, divide mixture into three equal portions in different bowls. To one add a few drops of red food colouring to give a pretty colour, not too pale and certainly not too bright. For the second portion, mix 2 tablespoons sifted cocoa with 2 tablespoons boiling water and 1 tablespoon sugar and cook stirring constantly over low heat until smooth. Allow to cool before adding to second portion of mixture with a tablespoon of sifted cornflour to compensate for the additional liquid. The third portion remains plain. For a rainbow or layer cake, bake each portion in a separate prepared sandwich pan for 25–30 minutes or until cakes test "done" with a skewer. For a marbled effect, put large spoonfuls of different colours alternately into a round cake tin or loaf tin. When all mixture is in, run a knife through once or twice so the colours intermingle in interesting patterns. Bake for 1 hour, covering with brown paper or foil for last 15 minutes of cooking, and test with skewer.

XII

MOTHER'S DAY

f I were to buy her all the flowers in the world on Mother's Day I could not repay what my mother does for me all year round. She has, I think, come to accept (tidy soul though *she* is) that her only daughter is unable to work except in a state of utter chaos, desk littered with scraps of paper, every one of which is precious.

She knows too that while inspiration flows and recipes are created in a kitchen so small that major traffic problems are inevitable, unless she comes to the rescue now and then the pile of baking tins and moulds and measuring cups and used dishes will get out of hand. I do it when she isn't there, but oh, how it helps when she is!

Mum is the most honoured guest at every party in our home, and the one who stays behind to help clear up. Mum is the one I can depend on to baby sit or pick up a child from school. Mum can massage a stiff shoulder or soothe a headache or bring cups of comforting brew to a sickbed, and is the best person to have around when flu or some such lays me low. She doesn't fuss, she just is there.

I'm not for Mother's Day, really. It is too glib a thing to bring a bunch of white chrysanthemums and a gift and forget mother for the rest of the year. I've seen it with older people. Families grown up and gone away, and only the occasional visit and, of course, the big hoo ha on Mother's Day.

Every day should be Mother's Day. Every day should be Father's Day. Every day should be Children's Day. Families are very special and we should relish every moment.

I hate breakfast in bed. In fact, I'm not big on breakfast at all, so heaven preserve me from cups of tea and toast crumbs under the blankets on Mother's Day. No, I'd rather wait till a civilised hour and enjoy the hot bagels my husband loves to make. Bagels spread with cream cheese and topped with smoked salmon. Not the sort of thing one can do too often, but now and then it just hits the spot!

Bagels

This is a rapid-mix method, using water much hotter than the lukewarm water used in the traditional method. But it is only dried yeast that can stand the higher temperature (around 54°C, 130°F), so don't try to hurry your yeast mixture along if using fresh compressed yeast.

Put 3 cups plain (all purpose) flour into a large bowl with 1 sachet active dry yeast, 3 tablespoons sugar and 2½ teaspoons salt. Stir to mix. Add 1½ cups very warm water (54°C, 130°F) all at once and mix well. This may be done on an electric mixer using a suitable attachment (not whisk). Mix in a further 1½ cups flour or enough to form a soft dough. Knead on a lightly floured board until smooth and elastic, adding only enough flour to keep the dough from sticking to hands. Put dough into a warm greased bowl and turn over once to grease top, then cover and put into a sink of hot water, or a warmed but turned-off oven, for 15–20 minutes. By this time the dough should have risen enough to hold an impression when two fingers are gently pressed into it.

Punch down dough, divide into four equal portions then divide each portion into four balls. Roll each ball to form a rope about 1.5 cm (½ inch) thick, moisten ends slightly and press firmly together to form a ring. (My unconventional husband prefers to form the shape by sticking his index finger through the middle of a ball of dough and twirling it until it becomes a ring. Men really are little boys at heart. Be careful if you try this — it is all too easy for the dough to fly off into space like one of Saturn's rings gone astray.)

Place the rings on lightly floured baking sheets and let stand in a warm place, covered with a tea towel, for 15 minutes. Meanwhile, set oven to moderate (170°C, 350°F), and bring a large pan containing at least 4 litres of water to the boil. When water boils gently slip 3 or 4 bagels into the pan (allow plenty of space) and simmer covered for about 5 minutes. Lift out with a slotted spoon and drain on a towel, then place on ungreased baking sheets. As soon as a tray is filled, brush bagels with beaten egg and sprinkle with poppy seeds. Bake for 25 minutes until golden. Remove and cool on rack. Serve warm, if possible, accompanied by cream cheese and lox (smoked salmon).

Compliment

He's small and chubby and not quite three,
and do you know what he said to me?
I was snuggling him down in his little bed
when, indistinctly, it was said,
and I didn't quite hear it when first it came.
"What's that, son?" So he said it again,
teeth clenched on his comforter, and once more
I couldn't hear it. (Yes, I know
three's old for a dummy, but they're better than thumbs,
and he only has it when bedtime comes.)
"Take that thing from your mouth and tell me again."
A dimpled hand moved the dummy, he said it plain
and clearly this time. At last I'd heard.
I'm ever so happy I persevered.
Just two small words, quite out of the blue
and for no good reason that I knew . . . .
"You're nice."
What made him say it? I'll never know,
but no words have ever moved me so.

My heart glows and I wear them all night and all day
as proudly as jewels or a lover's nosegay.

"You're nice." Small words, and only two.
I hope he'll always think they're true.

Thank you for My Mother

Dear God, thank you for my mother.
We have just been away on a holiday and,
as always,
she came and fed the dog,
watered the plants,
minded the house;
and when we came back
everything was clean and shining
and there were fresh flowers.
She knows it won't stay that way for long
once we, untidy mob that we are, get home,
but she does it anyway, bless her.
I do appreciate her help,
her willingness, her energy,
the way she organises things I never get around to
(like the linen cupboard).
Help me be more vocal, more demonstrative;
to find it easier to hug her and say,
"I love you, Mum."

ANSWER to a QUESTION

You ask me why I hold this man so dear,
and so I stop to ask myself. It's clear
I do, for he's the sun that lights my sky,
but until now I've never wondered why.

Is it the well-matched mind, comforting hands,
the passionate flame and sweetness of desire,
the reaching out for something better, higher?
Is it the moments shared in quietness,
remembering now and then some youthful, gay,
long past and unregretted, carefree day?
Is it the prayerful hope for our tomorrows,
hope for a twilight peaceful, shared and good,
blest children grown to man and womanhood,
and rest together after years of toil?

Ah yes, 'tis these and more, oh, so much more.
The worship shared. The laughter, tears and pain.
Even hot words that clear the air like rain.
The quiet togetherness true marriage knows.
There are so many reasons why love grows
within my heart, like some sweet-scented rose
sheltered and nurtured by his love for me.
In love! Oh, what a lovely way to be.

XIII
FATHER'S DAY

My father was a great story teller. I suspect, looking back, that his stories were somewhat dramatised for my benefit, but no doubt had at least a grain of truth in them. On hunting expeditions in the tropical forests of Ceylon he had his share of encounters with wild animals. While details escape me, I recall listening with fascination to his tales of hairbreadth escapes and breathtaking exploits.

He was a gregarious man and had many friends of different backgrounds, so I was totally unprepared for his reaction when I told him I was in love with a Jewish musician and that this same Jewish musician wanted to meet him and ask for my hand in marriage. I might as well have said I wanted to marry a Martian!

Father came from a staunchly Christian, utterly staid family, so my being courted by a musician was bad enough. But a musician who was also a Jew! In the little island of Ceylon, Jews were such an unknown quantity that there wasn't even a synagogue. Our small Burgher community, with its strict Dutch Reformed Church outlook, would be rocked like a boat in a tidal wave if my father's only child were to plunge into such a union.

He forbade it. He wouldn't even meet the prospective suitor. He . . . . oh well, that's all water under the bridge. Let me just say that he relented sufficiently to give the bride away, having discovered, once they met, that he really liked the stranger in our midst. As so often happens, he became firm friends with his son-in-law and was besotted with his grandchildren.

Now for the other father in my life — the father of my children. He is gentle and loving and a good provider, but can't remember the children's birthdays. He too has done his share of stalking game, but is afraid to hold a baby until it is old enough to sit up on its own. He will help me by shopping, cooking and cleaning, but I don't think he ever once pinned a nappy on one of our offspring.

I love his gift for music. It amazes and humbles me that this man who has occupied first chair (clarinet) in two symphony orchestras and has played lead saxophone with dance bands in four countries will play along with my stumbling piano accompaniment and never utter an impatient word. Love is not only blind, it must be deaf too!

I'm glad he can see the funny side of things and often makes me laugh just when we've got a good, healthy argument going. But we don't argue about religion. Palms spread upwards in a mischievous parody of that well-known Jewish gesture, he says with a grin, "After all, Christ was one of our boys!"

I learned about Jewish dietary laws so that I could entertain our relatives, both orthodox and liberal, and I have delighted in some of the traditional dishes associated with special feasts.

One of our favourites is *challah* (pronounced "hal-lah"), the Sabbath bread which is made with oil and eggs and shaped into a braid. Our daughter Deborah makes it really well, sweetening it with honey instead of sugar which is more commonly used. Glazed and sprinkled with poppy seeds, it is baked until golden-brown, filling the house with the fragrance that belongs to yeast breads alone. No-one can resist it, and we pull it apart while warm rather than cut it.

Challah

This quantity makes two good-sized loaves. Dissolve 30 g (1 oz) fresh compressed yeast or 1 sachet active dry yeast in 1 cup lukewarm water in a large mixing bowl. Stir in 1 teaspoon salt, $\frac{1}{4}$ cup honey, $\frac{1}{3}$ cup oil or melted butter and 2 lightly beaten eggs. Sift twice, $2\frac{1}{2}$ cups plain (all purpose) flour and 1 tablespoon gluten flour (the gluten can be left out, but it does make for a better-shaped loaf). Mix flour into bowl and beat very well with a wooden spoon or electric mixer for 5 minutes, or until stretchy and smooth. Add a further 2 cups flour, one cup at a time. Scatter $\frac{1}{2}$ cup flour onto a board, turn dough onto it and knead for 8–12 minutes or until smooth and elastic. Place dough in a greased bowl, turn it over so top is greased, then cover and put into a sink of hot water or a warm but turned-off oven for 15–20 minutes. By this time the dough should have risen enough to hold an impression when two fingers are gently pressed into it.

Punch down dough, divide in half and then divide each half into three equal pieces. Squeeze, roll and shape each piece into a strand about 2.5 cm (1 inch) thick. Place three of the strands side by side on a greased baking tray and start plaiting them together from the middle (this gives a more even plait). Turn tray around and plait the other end. Repeat with remaining dough on another tray. Cover with tea towels and let stand in a warm place until doubled in size again. Brush with beaten egg and sprinkle with poppyseeds. Preheat oven to moderate (170°C, 350°F). Bake loaves for 35–40 minutes or until they are well browned and sound hollow when tapped on the base. Slide onto a wire rack to cool.

Reuben's special kebab marinade

Fathers love to barbecue, and Reuben is no exception. He is very adventurous, and in this recipe combines ingredients from the Near and Far East, Hungary and Italy, with scant regard for cultural conflict. All I can say is, it tastes wonderful!

Put into container of electric blender 2 whole stalks fresh coriander (cilantro), 4 well-washed spring onions or scallions, 2.5 cm (1 inch) piece fresh ginger, peeled and roughly chopped, 1 clove garlic, and $\frac{1}{4}$ cup water. Blend until everything is very finely ground. Pour into a bowl and add 1 teaspoon paprika, 1 teaspoon Indian *garam masala* (available at Asian specialty food stores), $1\frac{1}{2}$ teaspoons salt, $\frac{1}{2}$ teaspoon dried oregano, 1 tablespoon soy sauce, 1 tablespoon vegetable oil, 2 teaspoons oriental sesame oil and $\frac{1}{4}$ cup ground rice. Combine thoroughly.

For **Kebabs**: Cut grilling steaks or lean lamb in 2.5 cm (1 inch) cubes and mix well with marinade. Cover and leave in refrigerator overnight, or at room temperature for at least 2 hours. Thread onto skewers and cook over glowing coals or under griller until well done. This marinade also goes well on chops, steaks, poultry or fish. The ground rice can be omitted, but gives a nice crisp effect.

XIV

THANKSGIVING

We were visiting America for the first time and planned it so we could spend Thanksgiving there. Little did I anticipate the events that would make it a time to remember.

We were looking forward to a reunion with my husband's brother in San Francisco. They are a loving, loyal family—these brothers and sisters really care about one another, and though they are scattered all over the globe, in England, America, Israel and Australia, they keep in touch and try to visit. On this visit the American branch of the family planned a tour of California on which they would accompany us so that we could enjoy the scenery and each other's company at the same time.

We were motoring down to Los Angeles from San Francisco. It was a bright, sunny autumn day and the whole world was wonderful. That night in our motel my husband woke with a pain in his chest. Circumventing all the details, let me just say that when we did get him to hospital (the nearest was sixty-five kilometres away) we found he had suffered a heart attack.

Abruptly, plans were changed. We booked into a motel in the small city of San Luis Obispo. Reuben's brother, who had suffered a heart attack ten years before and had recovered to lead a normal life, was a tower of strength. Thankfully, this attack was only a moderate one. After the first forty-eight hours which, the doctors warned, would be the critical period, we felt the others should go on with the tour and persuaded them to do so.

Much to our surprise, both Reuben and I found that the weeks that followed were the most peaceful we had experienced in a long time. Pressures of both work and the pursuit of pleasure were lifted. All he had to do was relax and let his heart heal itself. For me, it was an eye-opener. I learned that I could be self-reliant, make decisions, be alone in a strange country and cope. For so long I had depended on my husband to be with me wherever we went, and now I had to manage on my own. But I had help. That first night, after leaving the hospital, I telephoned my faithful friends and prayer partners in Australia.

"Little did I think," I said, "that someday we'd be praying across the Pacific Ocean." There is no distance in prayer. Across the miles we prayed and I know God answered. Reuben made a good recovery and I received a strength I could hardly believe. I have to confess that I am one of those born worriers. I don't want to be, but that's how I am. For me to have this freedom from anxiety in the midst of such a situation, this assurance and peace of mind, it had to be a miracle. Suddenly I was able to let go and let God take charge. When circumstances overwhelm, it is the only thing to do.

And so it was that when, a few weeks later, we gathered for Thanksgiving dinner, our hearts were full. The meal we partook of had been lovingly contributed to by each of the families present, and included all sorts of personal favourites in addition to the traditional roast turkey, cranberry relish and candied yams. This Pecan Pie was my contribution.

SAN LUIS OBISPO
FRIDAY, OCTOBER 31st 1980

Thank you, Lord, for your gentle care.
What happened could have been much worse,
but you brought us to a good hospital,
a good doctor.
You prepared the way before us
though it was not a path we would willingly have trod.

Thank you, Father, for sparing my darling's life.
And thank you for this lesson you are teaching me,
I who am always trying to be in control,
worrying about everything and everyone.
You brought me to a place where, helpless,
I simply had to let go and let you take charge.

Dear Lord, may I not forget this time,
this knowledge that the Eternal God is our refuge
and underneath are the everlasting arms.

Pecan pie

Sift 1½ cups plain (all purpose) flour and ½ teaspoon salt into a bowl, then rub in 125 g (4 oz) butter with fingertips. Add 2–3 tablespoons ice-cold water one tablespoon at a time until mixture holds together when gathered into a ball. Wrap pastry in plastic and chill for 20 minutes.

Prepare filling by creaming 2 tablespoons butter with ¾ cup brown sugar until light, then add pinch of salt, ½ cup dark corn syrup, 4 large, slightly beaten eggs and 1 teaspoon vanilla essence.

Roll out pastry and line a 22.5 cm (9 inch) pie plate. Prick base of pastry with a fork, line with a square of foil or greaseproof paper and weigh down with raw rice or beans. Bake in a preheated hot oven (200°C, 400°F) for 8 minutes. Lift out foil and rice or beans. Arrange 1 cup pecan halves in the partially baked pie shell and pour filling mixture over. Reduce oven heat to moderate (170°C, 350°F) and bake for 35 minutes or until a knife inserted in the centre comes out clean. Cool.

The Sick Child

Lord, I am only his mother.
You are his creator.
He grew within my body and I bore him,
but you, Lord, you fashioned him
and he is fearfully and wonderfully made.
Lay your hand upon him, Lord,
on the little body racked with pain.
Take away this sickness and the cause of it,
for ill health is not your will.
When you were on this earth you made this very clear,
for you went about healing the sick,
doing the will of your Father in heaven.
And, Lord, when the tempter says,
"Do you think he'll hear you
when there is so much going on in the world
of more importance than a sick child?",
I can dismiss him by calling to mind your words
when the disciples tried to spare you
from the demands of those mothers long ago:
"Suffer the little children
to come unto me, and forbid them not.
For of such is the kingdom of heaven."

XV
INVALID COOKERY

In most cookbooks there is a woeful lack of recipes for invalids— the sort of thing the doctor means when he prescribes "a light but nourishing diet". Having had more than my fair share of childhood illnesses I remember well the drinks on which I was sustained through bouts of fever and the foods on which I was nursed back to health.

How many mothers today know about Albumen Water, that marvellous aid to curing tummy troubles? And how many realise how simple it is to make a nourishing Chicken Broth ("Jewish penicillin" as it has been called), the old-fashioned cure-all especially favoured by Yiddisher mommas?

Can you make a Rice Gruel or Agar-agar Jelly for a patient with a funny tummy that is not so funny at all? The pain and sickness have passed, but any attempt to eat real food brings back the symptoms. Yet the patient is hungry and demanding something to eat. I hope you don't have to use these recipes too often, but for those occasions when they are necessary you may find them useful.

Remedies for upset tummies

Check with your doctor as to which is best for your patient.

Albumen Water: Take the white only of a fresh egg, put it into a cup or cereal bowl, add 1 teaspoon sugar and proceed to break up the gel by cutting repeatedly with a knife, or using a mashing movement with a fork, until it is quite liquid. Don't beat the egg white or you'll make it frothy and that's not what is needed here. Add 1 cup cool boiled water and just enough lemon juice to flavour. Stir well, strain through a fine sieve or piece of muslin. Add ice if liked and let the patient sip it slowly.

Whey: Heat 2 cups milk and as it starts to rise in the pan add 2 tablespoons lemon juice and stir. Remove from heat as soon as the milk separates into curds and whey. Let it stand for 5 minutes, then pour through a fine strainer or muslin. Sweeten whey to taste, and serve hot or cold.

Arrowroot Jelly: Mix 2 teaspoons arrowroot with a little water until smooth. In a small saucepan bring 1 cup water to the boil and stir in 2 teaspoons sugar. Pour in arrowroot stirring all the time and boil, stirring until clear. Flavour with 1 teaspoon lemon juice and colour a delicate pink with a few drops of red food colouring. Serve cold.

Grated Apple: Just after arriving in Australia I had a rather sick little girl on my hands. The lady doctor we consulted told me to give her grated apple left to go brown. To my mind this was an outlandish notion, and though I didn't say anything my look of startled disbelief must have been eloquent enough. This understanding physician said, "Here, read about it," and handed me a book on children's illnesses and the appropriate treatments.

I've found over the years that this is a most effective cure for simple gastric upsets, but (as always) check first with your family doctor.

Peel and grate an apple on a spotlessly clean grater, then leave it exposed to the air to go brown. Some varieties brown in a few minutes, others take a little longer. Sweeten with a little honey to make it more tempting.

For relief from nausea

Mace Water: Put 2 blades mace and 2 cloves into a cup or jug and pour over 1 cup boiling water. Cover with a saucer and allow to steep until cold. Strain, and let patient sip it slowly.

For relief from colds and fevers

Coriander and Ginger Tea: It saves time if a quantity of coriander seed is well washed, drained and dried in the sun or in a slow oven, then stored in an airtight tin or bottle.

Roast 3 tablespoons of cleaned coriander seed in a dry saucepan, stirring until the seeds smell fragrant. Add 2 cups water. Peel and slice a thumb-sized piece of fresh ginger, add it to the pan, cover and simmer for 15 minutes. Strain, sweeten to taste and serve very hot.

For relieving a stuffy nose, the steam is used as an inhalation. The patient leans over a bowl containing the coriander brew, a towel enveloping all, and breathes through the vapours.

For patients on semi-solid diets

Rice Gruel: Rice is a completely non-allergenic grain. Put 2 tablespoons washed white rice into a saucepan, add 2 cups water and cook for at least 1 hour or until rice is extremely soft. Strain and serve the liquid, seasoned with a pinch of salt or a little sugar. For patients on the mend, the rice itself may be mashed and offered with the liquid.

Agar-agar Jelly: A highly refined form of agar-agar, which is a seaweed, is sold at healthfood shops and Asian stores. Use 1 teaspoon agar-agar powder to each cup of water. Sprinkle agar-agar over boiling water in a pan and simmer, stirring, for a few minutes until all the agar-agar has dissolved. Sweeten to taste and flavour with a few drops of vanilla or rose essence. Colour a pale pink or green. Pour quickly into a small mould and allow to set. Agar-agar will set without refrigeration at a temperature of up to 27°C (80°F). For a softer jelly, use less agar-agar.

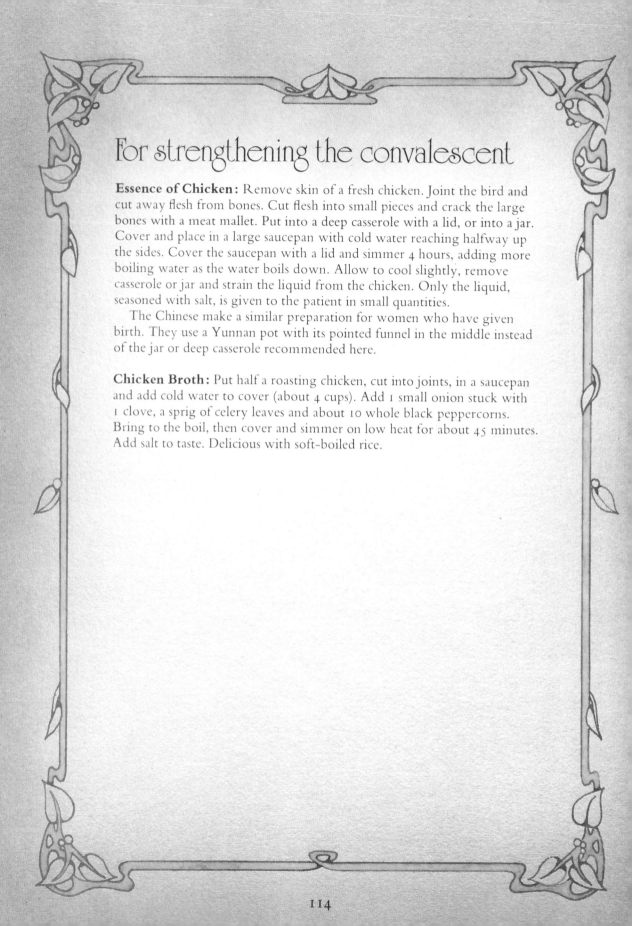

For strengthening the convalescent

Essence of Chicken: Remove skin of a fresh chicken. Joint the bird and cut away flesh from bones. Cut flesh into small pieces and crack the large bones with a meat mallet. Put into a deep casserole with a lid, or into a jar. Cover and place in a large saucepan with cold water reaching halfway up the sides. Cover the saucepan with a lid and simmer 4 hours, adding more boiling water as the water boils down. Allow to cool slightly, remove casserole or jar and strain the liquid from the chicken. Only the liquid, seasoned with salt, is given to the patient in small quantities.

The Chinese make a similar preparation for women who have given birth. They use a Yunnan pot with its pointed funnel in the middle instead of the jar or deep casserole recommended here.

Chicken Broth: Put half a roasting chicken, cut into joints, in a saucepan and add cold water to cover (about 4 cups). Add 1 small onion stuck with 1 clove, a sprig of celery leaves and about 10 whole black peppercorns. Bring to the boil, then cover and simmer on low heat for about 45 minutes. Add salt to taste. Delicious with soft-boiled rice.

XVI
MORNING

I'm not really a morning person. "There are owls and fowls," as one of my friends says. She's a fowl. I'm definitely an owl. I love sitting writing late at night after everyone's asleep. Or taking advantage of the late-night peace in the kitchen to stir a batch of jelly or put together a recipe that requires concentration.

But there are times when I have to be out of character and wake up with the birds, and on these occasions I am rewarded by seeing the world fresh and brightly shining as a new-minted coin. At these times I feel I should change my ways and see more early mornings than I do.

Something that makes me jump out of bed quick smart is the thought of cooking something really special and delicious for breakfast, to rouse sleeping children. I specially like muffins or waffles, for while they smell tantalising and lure the sleepy-heads from their beds they are also very easy and quick to make and healthy to eat.

Here are a few of our favourite morning recipes, including Fruity Bran Muffins. One of the nice things about them is that if any are left over they reheat well for afternoon tea.

Fruity bran muffins

This quantity makes about 12 muffins. Preheat oven to hot (200°C, 400°F). Sift into a large bowl 1 cup wholemeal flour, $\frac{1}{3}$ cup self-raising flour, 1 teaspoon baking soda (bicarbonate of soda), $\frac{1}{2}$ teaspoon baking powder and $\frac{1}{4}$ teaspoon salt. In a small saucepan melt 60 g (2 oz) butter, then remove from heat and add $\frac{1}{4}$ cup raw sugar, 1 lightly beaten egg and $\frac{1}{2}$ cup buttermilk or ordinary milk. Stir until sugar dissolves, then add $\frac{1}{2}$ teaspoon vanilla essence.

Add 1 cup bran cereal to liquid and allow to stand a few minutes until bran softens. Stir bran mixture into sifted ingredients with 1 cup diced ripe banana, apple or chopped dates, mixing quickly with a fork just enough to moisten the flour.

Put large tablespoons of mixture into greased muffin pans to three-quarters full, then bake in a hot oven for 25 minutes or until well-risen and golden. Serve warm with butter or as a special treat serve them with butter whipped and sweetened with honey.

As variations, you could replace the diced fresh fruit with dried fruits or frozen blueberries, or stir into plain unsweetened batter some crumbled, crisp-cooked bacon for savoury muffins.

French toast

Thank goodness for French toast! It's the easy, pleasant way to get an egg and milk and bread and butter into a child who's playing choosy at breakfast time. I've made this so often I could do it in my sleep!

Beat an egg with $\frac{1}{2}$ teaspoon sugar and a few drops of vanilla essence (do this in a large, flat dish like a pie plate so you can soak the bread in the same dish). Add about 3 tablespoons milk. Soak two slices of bread, cut in fingers, triangles or any shape you please, first on one side, then on the other. This should take up all the egg mixture. Heat a teaspoon of butter in a frying pan, fry bread until golden on one side, then turn and fry until golden on the other side. Serve sprinkled with cinnamon sugar, or spread with jam —you'll never see anything disappear so fast! Most children will even accept wholemeal bread when it's presented this way.

Waffles

If you have a waffle iron and are not using it often (this sometimes happens in our house too) why not unearth it, dust it down, and give the family a treat? Waffles are good not only at breakfast but at any time. If you don't have a waffle iron, cook as pancakes on a heated griddle or in a heavy frying pan.

Sift 2 cups self-raising flour with 1 teaspoon baking powder and $\frac{1}{2}$ teaspoon salt. If using plain (all purpose) flour instead of self-raising, use $2\frac{1}{2}$ teaspoons baking powder.

Separate 3 eggs. Beat yolks lightly, then mix in $1\frac{1}{2}$ cups milk and 3.tablespoons melted butter. Add all at once to the dry ingredients and beat vigorously until batter is smooth. Shortly before cooking, beat the egg whites until stiff and fold in.

Heat your waffle iron for about 6 minutes before you are ready to use it. Grease it if the surface is not non-stick, then ladle about $\frac{1}{2}$ cup batter into centre of iron. Close lid and cook until golden-brown.

My favourite way of eating waffles is hot from the iron, topped with a scoop of vanilla ice cream, a drizzle of syrup or honey, and a lavish sprinkling of chopped nuts.

Double-toasted granola

This recipe will give you 16 half-cup servings. Make ahead and store airtight.

Preheat oven to moderate (170°C, 350°F). Lightly oil a large roasting pan. Toast 125 g (4 oz) sesame seeds in a dry frying pan over low heat until golden, stirring all the time and shaking pan to prevent burning. When golden (this takes only about 3 minutes) turn seeds into a large bowl. In same pan toast 125 g (4 oz) sunflower seeds for the same length of time. Add to sesame seeds.

Put 125 g (4 oz) unblanched almonds into pan and shake over heat for 2 or 3 minutes. Cool slightly then put into a plastic bag and crush with the base of a stout bottle (don't put nuts through a food processor or blender — large, toasty pieces make the granola nicer and more crunchy). Repeat process with 60 g (2 oz) hazelnuts, toasting them in the pan for a slightly longer time. Rub in a tea towel and most of the skins should come off, then crush as you did the almonds and add both to bowl with sesame and sunflower seeds.

Stir in 4 cups rolled oats, $\frac{3}{4}$ cup wheatgerm and $\frac{3}{4}$ cup unprocessed bran. Combine well. Measure into a small pan $\frac{1}{4}$ cup oil, then $\frac{1}{2}$ cup honey (if you measure the oil first the honey won't stick to the cup) and heat gently until honey is liquid. Pour over ingredients in the bowl and mix thoroughly.

Spread half the mixture in a greased roasting pan and bake in a moderate oven for 15 minutes. Stir after the first 5 minutes and again after 10 minutes to prevent browning unevenly. Turn into a large bowl to cool, and repeat with other half of ingredients. Cool completely and store airtight. Serve in half-cup portions with milk, yoghurt or fresh fruit.

The Sparrow

Look, Lord, outside my kitchen window
there's a sparrow in a tree.
It sings and chirps so joyfully
and picks at the bark so busily
that it fills me with happiness.
It's early, and everyone else is still asleep.
I've got to share it with someone,
so I'm drawing your attention to it.

Thank you that it's here outside *my* window.
A sparrow isn't strictly necessary to my day,
but you sent it anyway.
My cup runneth over.

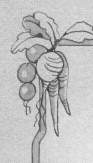

XVII
A ROMANTIC MEAL FOR TWO

Gougère

I used to do a lot of cooking late at night. I suppose this made sense, because my musician husband would come home after midnight starving hungry and I always had an appreciative audience for my efforts. I remember the first time I cooked *gougère*, it came out of the oven after midnight, all crisp and crusty and golden-brown, and smelling wonderful. We're not great wine drinkers, but as this is traditionally served with burgundy we broke into a bottle of the best red and sat sipping and supping and talking in the quiet of the house with all the children asleep.

The next time you go to the theatre, instead of rushing through your meal before you set out, arrange to have a quiet supper afterwards. And you could make a *gougère* (beforehand of course), put it in the refrigerator, then just pop it in the oven to cook when you return. A green salad is all the accompaniment you need. The quantity given here is enough for two, or for four as an entrée.

Preheat oven to moderately hot (190°C, 375°F). Put ½ cup milk or water into a heavy-based saucepan and add 60 g (2 oz) butter, ½ teaspoon dry mustard, ½ teaspoon salt and pinch white pepper. Bring to the boil. Meanwhile, sift ½ cup plain (all purpose) flour onto a sheet of greaseproof paper. When milk is boiling and butter is completely melted, add the flour all at once and stir briskly with a wooden spoon over medium heat until mixture forms a ball and leaves the sides of the pan. Remove from heat.

Lightly beat 2 eggs. Set aside in a cup about 1 tablespoon of the beaten egg, then beat the rest into the flour mixture a tablespoon at a time, beating well after each addition so that it is properly incorporated. Dough will be smooth and shiny.

Finely dice 60 g (2 oz) Emmenthal or Gruyère cheese. Set aside a handful and fold the rest into pastry mixture. Use a buttered tablespoon to put lumps of dough the size of an egg on a well-buttered baking tray. Arrange them, just touching each other, in a circle about 15 cm (6 inches) across. With a teaspoon put smaller portions of dough on top of the larger ones. Brush a light coating of reserved beaten egg over the pastry, taking care egg does not drip down onto the baking tray. Lightly press the remaining diced cheese onto the *gougère*.

Bake in a moderately hot oven for 10 minutes, then lower heat to moderate (170°C, 350°F) and bake a further 30 minutes. Pastry should puff up and be a rich golden-brown colour. Serve hot, using two forks to separate the portions.

If making ahead of time, shape raw pastry on baking tray, lightly cover with plastic wrap and put in refrigerator. Brush with egg and sprinkle with cheese before baking.

More precious than Diamonds

"He crowneth me with loving kindness . . ."
Lord, I hope you won't mind if I borrow those words
that David the psalmist said about you.
But they so exactly describe how I feel
about the way my husband treats me. "He crowneth me
with loving kindness."

And yet, Lord, do you know what?
The dear, foolish man worries.
Worries because he hasn't crowned me with diamonds
and clothed me in mink and sable.
Where do men get the notion that all women
secretly hanker for these things?
Really, Lord, I wouldn't want them even if we could afford them.
I've told him, yet he feels a failure
because we don't have unlimited money and luxurious living.
But I wouldn't change places with anyone,
and I mean *anyone*!
I think of the times he has taken over in the kitchen
or helped clean the house
or brought me a cup of coffee in bed
or done so many things to help when I,
in my usual impulsive fashion,
take on more than I can handle.

Oh yes, I can live without wealth, but I cannot live
without the loving kindness,
the love.
I wear it like a shining coronet.
More precious than diamonds
and oh, so much more comfortable.

Afterglow

The pale gold dawning of our love
warms the sky with timid streaks
of light
and slowly turns
to passion's noontide.
The blazing sun
makes hot and bright
our whole world.
But sunset with its lingering warmth,
its skies flushed gold and crimson,
its flecks of burnished cloud
soon fading to a dove-breast grey
in which the eternal stars appear and shine
is,
I think,
the loveliest time of all.

XVIII
CELEBRATION SUPPER FOR TWENTY~FIVE

It's wonderful to have a special occasion to celebrate, to shine the silver, bring out treasured linen and spend recklessly on flowers.

I'm sharing with you a menu that I have used more than once, so I know it works particularly well for a large number. Everything except a green salad and the punch may be prepared well ahead of time and frozen, or a day or two ahead and refrigerated. It's the sort of food that doesn't mind waiting, and will comfortably feed twenty-five people at a buffet meal.

I dreamed it up for a supper to follow my older daughter's first concert recital, and since we would be spending the hours immediately prior to the party sitting in a theatre listening to her play, it had to be the sort of menu with no last-minute hassles.

Your occasion may be a birthday or an anniversary or a graduation party, or it may just be good friends gathered for no other reason than that it's good to be together, to appreciate the gifts of life and love and congenial company. Enjoy!

Caviar roll with sour cream

Imagine a soufflé that looks more like a sponge roll—that's what a *roulade* is. This one is served cold with a luxurious filling of caviar and cream cheese. It's ideal for a party because it is made well ahead. As this recipe is very much easier to handle in small quantities, I make *two* rolls, the second being made while the first is baking. The filling may be made in one lot.

Preheat oven to moderate (170°C, 350°F). Brush a Swiss-roll tin 25 × 37.5 cm (10 × 15 inches) with oil, line tin with greaseproof paper and brush the paper with oil. Sprinkle lightly with flour and shake to coat paper, then tip out excess flour.

Melt 60 g (2 oz) butter in a medium-sized saucepan, draw pan away from heat and add ½ cup plain (all purpose) flour. Stir over heat for a minute or two without letting the mixture brown. Remove from heat, add ½ teaspoon salt and whisk in 2 cups milk gradually. Return to heat and cook, stirring constantly, until sauce comes to the boil and is thick and smooth.

Remove the pan from heat. Separate 4 eggs. Beat into sauce 4 egg yolks one at a time. Stiffly beat 4 egg whites and stir a quarter of the whites into the mixture to lighten it, then quickly and gently fold in the remaining egg whites. Spread mixture in prepared tin and bake in a moderate oven until well-risen and golden, about 45 minutes.

While this roll is baking make up ingredients as above for second roll, but do not beat the egg whites yet. Make up caviar filling (page 134) and set aside.

Remove cooked roll from oven, turn out on a sheet of greaseproof paper and carefully peel off paper from base. Quickly trim off edges with a sharp knife. Spread the roll with half the caviar filling and roll up lengthwise, using the paper to lift the end of the roll. Put it seam down on a serving dish. Allow to cool.

If you don't have two Swiss-roll tins, wash and dry the tin and prepare it once more with oil, greaseproof paper and flour. Beat the 4 egg whites and fold into second batch of cooked sauce mixture. As before, spread mixture into prepared tin and bake in a moderate oven about 45 minutes, until risen and golden. Turn out as before and fill with remaining caviar filling. Put seam down on serving dish and allow to cool. Make sour cream sauce (page 134). Cover and chill both rolls.

To serve, cut in diagonal slices with a very sharp knife (an electric knife is an asset) and arrange the slices with their swirls of red caviar filling on a large platter lined with lettuce leaves. Garnish with sprigs of watercress or parsley. Hand the sour cream sauce separately.

Caviar Filling and Sour Cream Sauce: Beat 375 g (12 oz) cream cheese, softened to room temperature, until smooth. Add about 4 tablespoons thick sour cream, then fold in 185 g (6 oz) red caviar. Taste and add lemon juice and white pepper to accentuate the flavour. This is the filling.

Mix a further 185 g (6 oz) red caviar with 2½ cups sour cream and season with lemon juice and white pepper as required. Pile into a bowl and chill. Serve separately, to be spooned over individual servings.

Seafood crêpes

You may think this sounds like an awful lot of eggs to go into a crêpe batter, but having tried many recipes I find this one makes the finest, most tender crêpes. I've used the blender method for the batter, being the quickest and easiest — but you've got to remember to make it about two hours before you start cooking the crêpes so the batter can rest. I use a heavy cast-iron 12.5 cm (5 inch) crêpe pan. Electric crêpe makers need a slightly heavier batter than this, so if using one add an extra ¼ cup flour to the mixture.

Break 5 eggs into container of electric blender, add 1¼ cups each of milk and water and blend about 5 seconds. Add 1¼ cups plain (all purpose) flour and 1 teaspoon salt sifted together, and blend for about 10 seconds. Scrape down sides of blender, add 2 tablespoons melted butter and blend another 10 seconds until smooth. Strain batter through a fine nylon sieve into a large bowl and let rest for 2 hours.

Heat a heavy crêpe pan and grease very lightly with butter. Pour 2 tablespoons batter into the pan and swirl to coat evenly. Pour any excess batter back into bowl. Cook until golden on underside, turn over and cook for about 30 seconds on other side. Stack crêpes as they are made. If making crêpes well ahead of time, they may be stacked with squares of greaseproof paper between and frozen. Makes at least 25 crêpes.

Seafood Filling: Take 1 kg (2 lbs) scallops *or* raw prawns *or* white fish fillets *or* mixture of seafood. Wash scallops, remove brown vein, rinse again, dry well on kitchen paper, and cut in halves. If using prawns, remove shell and vein, chop into large pieces. Fish fillets too should be cut into pieces. Season with salt and pepper and lightly coat with flour, shaking off any excess.

Melt 60 g (2 oz) butter in a small pan on low heat and fry $\frac{1}{2}$ cup finely chopped spring onions just until soft. Pour in 1 cup dry vermouth, cover and simmer for 5 minutes. Heat 4 tablespoons olive oil with 60 g (2 oz) butter in a heavy frying pan and when very hot put in the seafood and sauté lightly on all sides for just a few minutes. Do not cook too long or seafood will toughen. Lift out with a slotted spoon, add to vermouth mixture in the pan and simmer gently for 3 minutes.

Cream Sauce: Melt 125 g (4 oz) butter in a saucepan. Add 8 tablespoons plain (all purpose) flour and stir over medium heat for 2 minutes. Remove from heat, add 2 cups hot milk and whisk with a wire whisk until smooth. Season to taste with salt and white pepper. Return to heat and stir until sauce bubbles, then remove from heat and stir in $\frac{1}{2}$ cup cream and prepared seafood filling.

Place a large spoonful of mixture on each crêpe, roll up, and place in a row on a buttered ovenproof dish. Cover with foil and bake in a preheated moderately hot oven (190°C, 375°F) about 25 minutes. Serve hot. If making ahead of time, place crêpes in dish, cover with foil and refrigerate. Bake just before serving time.

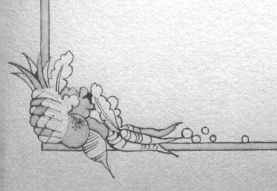

Terrine with chicken breasts

Choose a glass, earthenware or enamel ovenproof dish or casserole if you
haven't a terrine. Avoid using metal pans, which react with the meat juices
and wine and give the jelly a metallic taste.

Bone 3 large chicken breasts. Place the breasts on waxed paper on a wooden
board skin downwards, and use a meat mallet or rolling pin to flatten the
thickest portion slightly. They should not be beaten out thinly, just try to
make them an even thickness throughout.

Put 1.5 kg (3 lbs) minced veal in a large bowl. In a two-cup measure
sprinkle 1½ tablespoons gelatine over ½ cup cold water and set aside for 5
minutes to soften. Heat 90 g (3 oz) butter in a heavy-based saucepan and
cook 1½ cups finely chopped spring onions over a low heat until soft and
just starting to change colour, about 10 minutes. Add onions to meat in
bowl. In the same pan, heat 1 cup madeira or sherry, then pour over soaked
gelatine and stir to dissolve. Crush 1 small clove garlic with 1 teaspoon salt
and stir into wine mixture with 2 more teaspoons salt and 1 teaspoon each
of dried ground thyme, oregano, allspice and black pepper. Mixing the
seasonings into the wine is a good way to make sure they are well
distributed in the meat mixture.

Add wine mixture and 2 tablespoons whole green peppercorns (drained)
to meat and onions in the bowl and mix thoroughly. It is best to use your
hands. Line a large terrine or ovenproof casserole with the chicken breasts
skin side against the dish. Put in the meat mixture, season with salt and
freshly ground pepper and press down well. Cover with aluminium foil,
then with a lid. If the dish has no lid, use a double thickness of foil and fold
securely over the rim.

Place dish in a roasting pan on the middle shelf of the oven and pour in
boiling water to come halfway up the side of the dish. Bake in a moderate
oven (170°C, 350°F) for 1½ hours. The mixture will shrink slightly from
side of dish. Lift dish from the water and remove lid, leaving foil on the
top. Place a small board or plate which fits inside the dish over the foil and
place a weight on the board. This ensures that the texture of the loaf will
be compact and easy to slice. Leave to cool, then chill overnight before
removing weight.

To serve, turn out on serving dish and cut in slices, or serve it at the table
in the terrine, accompanied by crusty bread and a tossed green salad.

Hazelnut Sabra torte

I first made this torte for daughter Deborah's sixteenth birthday, when we surprised her with a dinner party. Since then it has been a family favourite for any kind of celebration. Because it is so rich it should be sliced thinly; this quantity will yield about 25 slices. An electric knife is ideal for cutting it neatly.

Put 500 g (1 lb) hazelnuts in a single layer in a shallow baking tray and bake in a slow oven (150°C, 300°F) for 15–20 minutes until pale golden. Allow to cool slightly, then rub hazelnuts in a clean dry towel to remove skins. It does not matter if some of the skins don't come off. Put cooled hazelnuts through the fine blade of a mincer, or grind a few at a time in electric blender, being careful not to overprocess or they will become oily. A nut grinder is ideal.

Prepare three baking trays. Line the trays with aluminium foil, brush with oil and dust with flour. Lightly mark a 25 cm (10 inch) circle in the flour. Preheat oven to moderately slow (160°C, 325°F).

In a large bowl which is very clean and dry (or the egg whites won't whip up well!) whisk 8 egg whites with 2 teaspoons vanilla essence and $\frac{1}{2}$ teaspoon cream of tartar until soft peaks form. Add $2\frac{1}{4}$ cups caster sugar gradually and continue beating until thick and glossy. An electric mixer helps a lot up to this point.

Now use a spatula or metal spoon to fold in the ground hazelnuts. Divide the mixture into three equal parts and spread each out to a 25 cm (10 inch) circle on the prepared trays. Bake for 30 minutes or until firm. You may have to bake one layer, or at the most two, at a time. Remove layers carefully from trays and peel off the foil from base. Leave on a wire rack to cool. If the circles have spread unevenly, transfer to a board and trim edges until they are uniform in size and shape. While the hazelnut layers are cooling make the butter-cream filling and chocolate cream (page 138).

(The nice thing about this type of recipe is that you can make the layers days ahead, wrap them in foil, and store airtight until needed. Make the filling ahead, too, and store in the refrigerator, well covered so the delicate butter cream cannot absorb any foreign flavours. Bring the filling to room temperature before using.)

Sandwich the layers together with the light butter-cream filling and cover top and sides of cake with the chocolate cream. Save a bit of each to pipe a decorative edge around top of cake using an icing bag fitted with a shell or star nozzle. This cake improves if assembled a day or two ahead, covered with foil, and refrigerated.

Sabra Butter-Cream Filling: Whisk 4 egg yolks with $\frac{1}{2}$ cup sugar and 2 teaspoons cornflour until thick and light. In a heavy saucepan heat $1\frac{1}{2}$ cups milk with 1 cup sugar until milk comes to the boil, stirring until sugar is dissolved. Pour the milk gradually onto the yolks, stirring constantly. Return mixture to pan and cook over very low heat, stirring briskly all the time, until mixture thickens enough to coat back of spoon with a thin custardy layer. This is usually done over simmering water but it takes a very long time and I'd rather cook it over direct heat, but you must be watchful. Don't allow the custard to boil or it will curdle. As soon as it thickens remove from heat, pour into a bowl and place in a sink of cold water, continuing to stir until it has cooled somewhat. Strain through a nylon sieve and refrigerate until very cold.

While custard cools, chop 200 g (7 oz) dark chocolate and put into a dry bowl. Place over a pan of hot (*not* boiling) water — remember that not a drop of moisture should be allowed near the chocolate, or it will seize up. Stir chocolate until it is melted and smooth, then allow to cool.

Cream 500 g (1 lb) butter until light, adding finely grated rind of 2 oranges and 4 tablespoons Sabra or other orange-flavoured liqueur. Gradually add the cold custard, a spoonful at a time, beating well until it has been incorporated (here again, an electric mixer is invaluable). Divide the cream into two equal portions, add the cooled chocolate to one and mix well. Fill and frost the hazelnut layers.

Party punches

For any large party the punch bowl is an ideal answer to the vexed question of what to serve to drink. I make a non-alcoholic fruit punch and a very light, sparkling champagne punch, and find that everyone likes one or the other. If you don't have two punch bowls (and they are a nuisance to find shelf space for between parties) just use a large salad bowl or even your largest mixing bowl. With ice and mint leaves and fruit floating in colourful array, no-one will mind that the container was not created with that purpose in mind. These recipes make 25 to 30 punch-cup servings.

Fruity Champagne Punch: You can use strawberries or peaches, or other fruit in season. Whatever fruit you use must be ripe and sweet but still quite firm so it can be cut into sharp-edged pieces and not go mushy or it will spoil the look of the punch. I like to use Grand Marnier, Cointreau or other good orange-flavoured liqueur for the strawberries, and peach brandy if using peaches.

Wash 2 punnets ripe strawberries, drain and hull them. Slice large strawberries or cut smaller berries in halves. Put them into a bowl, sprinkle with ¼ cup caster sugar and pour ½ cup liqueur over. Cover and chill for 2 hours.

If using peaches, put 4 firm peaches into a bowl and pour boiling water over them to cover, leave for 30 seconds, then drop peaches into ice-cold water. The skins should slip off easily. Rub over with lemon juice to prevent them discolouring. With a stainless steel knife cut the fruit into thin slices and then into dice and drop them into bowl containing ½ cup peach brandy. Add ¼ cup caster sugar. Cover and chill for 2 hours.

At serving time put the fruit mixture into a punch bowl, add 2 chilled bottles sauterne and stir gently to dissolve any remaining grains of sugar. Add a large block of ice rather than ice cubes, as it will dissolve more slowly and won't water down the punch too quickly.

Just before serving, add 1 or 2 chilled bottles champagne and 1 large bottle chilled soda water.

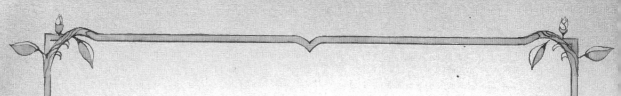

Spiced Tea Punch: A non-alcoholic punch for the sophisticated palate. It's light and refreshing, and just the thing if you have to drive afterwards.

Place 1 cup sugar in enamel or stainless steel saucepan, add 1½ cups water and heat until sugar is dissolved, stirring. Add 2 sticks cinnamon, 10 whole cloves and 4 cardamom pods. Heat to boiling, boil 5 minutes, then remove from heat and allow to cool.

Make a strong infusion of tea (3 tablespoons India or Ceylon tea in 6 cups boiling water) and leave to brew for 5 minutes. Strain into a large bowl. Strain syrup into same bowl, stir well and leave to cool. Add strained juice of 2 lemons and 3 or 4 oranges (use bottled fruit juice if no fresh is available) and slices of lemon and orange. Just before serving add ice cubes and chilled lemonade or soda water. Float tiny mint sprigs on top.

Pineapple Punch: This is a simple fruit punch, just right for children. Don't be surprised at the salt called for — you'll be amazed how a little salt brings out the flavour of the pineapple. If you have some fresh pineapple, add 1 cup of very finely chopped fruit.

Chill 1 large can unsweetened pineapple juice and 1 large bottle ginger ale. Peel, seed and finely dice 1 cucumber, then chill. Roughly chop a few sprigs of fresh mint. When all ingredients are really cold, mix together in chilled bowl with crushed ice. Stir ½ teaspoon salt into punch.

You might like to make a pretty wreath by arranging cherries and mint leaves in a ring tin, pouring water over and freezing it, or use orange juice or lemon juice instead of water. The ring floating in the punch looks most festive.

XIX
AS TIME GOES BY

I am thankful now for those first lonely years in a new country and for the homesickness that compelled me to write long letters to my mother. Thank goodness, too, for a mother who kept every letter. She doted on her grandchildren, and I felt awful taking them so far away, so I tried to share with her all the experiences I was having with them. The toddlers in these extracts from those old letters are young women now, but let's turn the clock back twenty years or so and eavesdrop a little—I'm sure every mother will recognise the joys, the pride, the tiredness and exasperation, and of course the rewards.

How I wish you were here to help with the little terrors. Debbie has started waking up every night and cries until I take her into bed with me. It is most uncomfortable because she monopolises the middle of the bed and I'm left out in the cold! I must try and break her of the habit. The moment she lays her head on my pillow she is angelically asleep, otherwise she howls like a banshee . . . . .

At three this morning they were both awake. At four Debbie started pulling Nina's hair, laughing in glee. She doesn't mean to hurt, just loves pulling hair. "Don't pull my hair, Debbie, that's not funny." Then, as Deb's mirth increased, she yelled again, "That's not funny!" One has to laugh. On the other hand, if I rebuke Debbie, she turns protector. I scolded Debbie for pulling cups and plates out of the cupboard and breaking something, but Nina reproached me with "Debbie's helping you, Mummy," and made me feel a tyrant.

Two and a half years old can be an exasperating age. This morning Nina did something silly and I said, "Don't be a silly ass." Quick as a wink came the reply, "I am not a silly ass, I'm is a NINA." She's using big words now, words like "perspiring" and "p'obably", and in the right places, too. Impressed, I said to her, "You're a marvel." Highly insulted, she replied, "I is not a marble, I'm a Nina Solomon." Great sense of identity she has, that kid.

Debbie is being distractingly helpful, banging the typewriter keys whenever I stop to think and generally "pestifying" me. She is such a smiler, Mum. Only this morning she was being very jolly and loveable and I hugged her and said, "How I wish your grandmother could share you." Suddenly she talks like a book. Sometimes, if she is in her cot and Reuben and I are talking in the next room, we hear a stern shout, "Wha's you talking about, you two?" Her "r's" are all "w's".

It is so funny, getting things that I say flung back at me. Early in the morning I heard an imperious voice from the cot, "Mummy, I wanna come to your bed." "Yes, darling, in a minute," I answered, more asleep than awake. "Not in a minute, right now!" came the reply.

Last night Nina was making a fuss about something and I said to her, "Don't be a fuss pot, darling, you know it's not as bad as you try to make out," and she said to me in tones of outraged virtue, "God and I know I'm not telling a lie."!! She surely cites the most reliable of witnesses.

Now, years later, we read and chuckle over those incidents. Nina has become a professional musician, Debbie a home economist. "One to play music with you, one to cook with me," I say to their father.

To earn her Bachelor of Music degree, Nina had to give a concert performance of not less than forty minutes. I well remember the night. Her Dad was so nervous I had to give him a sedative.

"She'll survive, you might not," I told him.

I shall never forget the thrill of listening to our daughter play Chopin, Beethoven and Mozart in a proper theatre. She played well, too. While she decided that to be a concert pianist demands more than she is prepared to sacrifice to a career, I shall always treasure the memory of that night.

Debbie too excelled as a student and in addition to getting her diploma won prizes in special subjects and won, too, the praise and affection of her teachers. Once again we had the privilege of watching our second daughter receive her diploma. A diploma or degree is no guarantee of success, I know, but it doesn't take away the thrill of being present at such an occasion.

In the kitchen, Debbie is quick and capable and sure of herself. Nina is not as practical but she can and does cook well, and loves doing the artistic bits like coating rose leaves with chocolate, using both dark and light chocolate for a two-tone effect. When we made our special hazelnut torte for Debbie's surprise party, Nina decorated it to look like a field of miniature mushrooms—made with meringues. But it was Debbie who made and iced Nina's twenty-first birthday cake, a beautiful pink and white creation with moulded roses, something I've never had the patience to persevere with.

This book is a gift for my husband in our silver wedding year, and for my children too. They may not have written any of the chapters, but are the reason for any of this having been written at all. It is my "song for tomorrow", a thought borrowed from the title of one of the songs Nina has written, and which I love so much that I've asked her to let me use it here (pages 150–151).

Two Daughters

Two daughters have I,
each different from the other as the night from day,
yet each one lovely in her own sweet way.

Nina is moonlight on a quiet pool,
Debbie is sunshine on a summer sea.
Nina is dark red roses, autumn leaves,
Debbie is daffodils dancing in the breeze.
Nina's a song in the stillness of the night,
Debbie the chorus of a laughing throng.
Nina is my firstborn, my joy and my delight;
Debbie the sweetest, gayest creature ever born.

Both are life and joy and light.
Both are born of tender love.
Both are daughters sweet and good.
Oh, the joys of motherhood!

SONG FOR TOMORROW

words and music by Nina Solomon

There's a song on the breeze, fal-ling down the sky from hea-ven Did a bird put it there just to bright-en my day? And the sky is so blue And my heart, it feels like dan-cing, It's a beau-ti-ful day and I'm here

There's a breeze in the trees, And it's made the leaves start spin-ning, And it's blow — ing my hair, And it makes me feel good, And the sun's in the sky, And the song-bird's fly-ing by me, And the sun on the wat-er's like gold And when I sing this song to all the child-ren They smile be - cause the words are

Make The Tree Tall

Make the tree tall,
for he is so small
and I want him to remember
the biggest, highest, sparkliest tree of all.

The trees of my childhood were always so big,
but as I've grown older they've kept getting smaller
and not so exciting, somehow.
Don't they grow trees as tall anymore?

Or could it be that the fault is in me?
The trees aren't too small, but I'm too big.
Too big to look upwards and be dazzled,
to see the shining star on the topmost branch
and wish I could touch it.
(Of course I can. I put it there.)

So for now, make the tree tall.
He is so small
and I want him to remember
the biggest, highest, sparkliest tree of all.

XX
WHEN CHRISTMAS COMES

Christmas is a time for remembering. At no other time of the year are good times as good or sad times as poignant.

Though the image of Christmas is inextricably merged with cold and snow, this is just not true for countries in the tropics or in the southern hemisphere, and that is where I've spent most of mine.

I recall vividly the one and only winter Christmas of my life. It was spent with friends in Lowestoft, the easternmost point of the British Isles, swept by winds that seemed to come straight from the Arctic Circle. In that cosy English cottage a blazing fire in the hearth warmed the room with its heavy oak beams and amid laughter and feasting nobody cared that snow clouds hung heavy in the sky. Roast turkey wreathed with tiny chippolata sausages, sage and onion stuffing, rich dark plum pudding and hot custard sauce made it a Christmas straight out of Dickens' *A Christmas Carol*.

Until I came to Australia where December means high summer and many people celebrate at beach picnics (now there's a contrast for you!), most of my Christmases were spent in Ceylon, just ten degrees north of the equator, or in Rangoon, Burma. Ceylon is predominantly Buddhist but the capital city, Colombo, would light up like a Christmas tree at the approach of this most joyous of Christian festivals. In the warm tropical nights shops stayed open till all hours and pavement vendors spread their array of toys and baubles on footpaths so one could hardly pick a path through without being tempted to buy far too many. Even when I was quite old enough to know better, I used to lay my pillowcase at the foot of my bed and the indulgent elders of the household would not disappoint me.

I remember too the first Christmas of our marriage—our best gift was knowing we would be parents the following July. And the excitement of Christmas with the children! I realise now that the brightly lit tree, the far too many gifts, were more for our pleasure than for that of the little one who could only just sit up and who almost fell over with surprise when the soft toy she grabbed retaliated by squeaking loudly.

Perhaps the happiest Christmases were when the children were old enough to appreciate the celebration yet young enough to be dazzled. Reuben's work as a musician kept him out till at least midnight even on Christmas Eve, so it would be the wee small hours before we could fill the children's pillowcases together. How we enjoyed doing that, and how exhausted we were when we fell into bed. It seemed my head had only just touched the pillow when I would be awoken by shrieks of joy from the children's room. One Christmas morning, in a state of sheer delight, one satisfied customer kept walking around the room shouting to the ceiling "Thank you, Santa!".

For most of us, memories are tied up with the scents and tastes of festive foods, so much a part of the tradition. If Christmas has a smell, I've often thought, it is surely the smell of pine trees and fruitcake. I love a real tree, its woody, resinous odour growing stronger each day and declaring "It's Christmas" as clearly as any carol. And fruitcake made at home, wafting its spicy fragrance through every part of the house, echoes "It's Christmas" just as unmistakably.

They are lovely, heart-warming smells, but smells that coming generations may never know as people succumb to the convenience of fruitcake bought in shops and everlasting trees made from tinsel and plastic that are folded away at the end of the season and taken out again the following year.

The eating of fruitcake is a treat, but the making of it is even more of a delight, the stuff of which memories are made. Our Christmas cake is always made to the same recipe, handed down from the Dutch ancestors on my father's side of the family. We make it in large quantities because we have so many visitors. Out comes the biggest boiler to do duty as a mixing bowl, and everybody gathers around for a stir and a wish.

To you all—at Christmas, Hanukkah, and all through the year— Shalom! Love and Peace!

Heirloom cake

If possible, make the fruit mixture as many as three days ahead of the cake mixture so that the fruits have time to macerate. You will need 375 g (12 oz) sultanas and 250 g (8 oz) each of seedless raisins, mixed glacé fruit, preserved ginger, and red glacé cherries. Make sure there are no tough stems among the sultanas, and pick the raisins over carefully—I don't really trust the "seedless" claim, and some of them are remarkably seedy, so press them with your fingertips to feel for seeds and remove any you find (there's nothing more devastating than biting down on a gritty seed). Chop sultanas and raisins. Cut the glacé fruit and preserved ginger into small pieces, and the whole glacé cherries into quarters as it is nice to see colourful bits of cherry through the cake.

Take 1 jar (410 g or 14 oz) Chinese chow chows in syrup, and cut chow chows into small pieces, retaining syrup. Alternatively use 500 g (1 lb) melon and ginger jam. Finely chop 125 g (4 oz) mixed peel. Chop 250 g (8 oz) raw cashews or blanched almonds, but not so finely that they become ground up and unrecognisable. Combine all fruits and nuts in a large bowl, pour over them any syrup from the chow chows or preserved ginger, and add ¼ cup brandy. Mix well. Cover tightly with plastic wrap and leave overnight or longer.

Line a 25 cm (10 inch) round or square cake tin, or two smaller tins, with two thicknesses each of newspaper and brown paper, then two layers of greaseproof paper, and brush greaseproof liberally with melted butter.

For the cake mixture, have 375 g (12 oz) butter at room temperature so it is easy to work. Cream butter with 500 g (1 lb) caster sugar until light. Add 12 egg yolks one at a time, beating well after each is added. Now add 2 teaspoons finely chopped lime or lemon rind; 1½ teaspoons ground cardamom, 1 teaspoon ground cinnamon, 1 teaspoon freshly grated nutmeg and ½ teaspoon ground cloves; 2 tablespoons vanilla essence, 1 tablespoon almond essence, 2 teaspoons rose essence, and 1 tablespoon honey. If you think these quantities for vanilla and almond are incredibly generous, just trust me and put them in anyway. In the finished cake they are not too strong at all, and make all the difference between this cake and others with their timid teaspoon of vanilla. Mix well, gradually adding 250 g (8 oz) medium semolina.

By now you have quite a large amount of mixture, so use your largest bowl or boiler. Add the prepared fruit and nut mixture, mixing it in with both hands (much easier than using a spoon, and this is the way professional bakers do it). When the fruit is thoroughly mixed in, whip 6 egg whites until stiff and stir through the mixture. Turn mixture into prepared tin or tins, and bake in a very slow oven (130°C, 275°F) for between 2½ and 4½ hours. The shorter baking time will give you a very moist cake, which is how some people (myself included) like it. The longer you bake it, the firmer it will become. Cover cake with paper or foil after the first hour to prevent overbrowning. Cool in the tin, leaving cake about 24 hours before turning out and wrapping tightly in foil. A tablespoon or two of brandy can be sprinkled over the cake before wrapping.

A week or so before using, ice with almond paste and fondant. But make the cake at least three weeks before to give it time to mature. This also makes a delicious wedding cake.

Whole fruit and nut cake

This is the cake to make when there is no time for the chopping and elaborate preparation that goes into the Heirloom Cake. Nothing could be quicker or easier, and while not as spicy or rich it is a spectacularly colourful cake with good keeping properties.

Line a loaf pan with aluminium foil and preheat oven to slow (150°C, 300°F). Put 250 g (8 oz) each of whole red and whole green glacé cherries in a bowl with 250 g (8 oz) mixed glacé fruit that has been cut into large pieces (if liked, fruits can be soaked overnight in ½ cup brandy or sherry). Toast 250 g (8 oz) hazelnut kernels in slow oven for 20 minutes, then rub off skins with a cloth. Add hazelnuts (or pecan halves) and 250 g (8 oz) brazil nut kernels to fruit. Sift ¾ cup sugar, 1 cup plain (all purpose) flour, 1 teaspoon baking powder and ¼ teaspoon salt over fruit mixture and toss well with hands to coat mixture evenly.

Beat 3 eggs with rotary beater until frothy, add 1 teaspoon vanilla essence and pour over fruit mixture. Stir well. Turn mixture into prepared loaf pan and bake in a slow oven for 1½–2 hours, covering cake with a square of foil after 30 minutes to prevent top browning too much. Cool cake in tin on wire rack. When cold, wrap in foil and leave at least a day or two (longer if possible) before cutting. It should be cut in very thin slices.

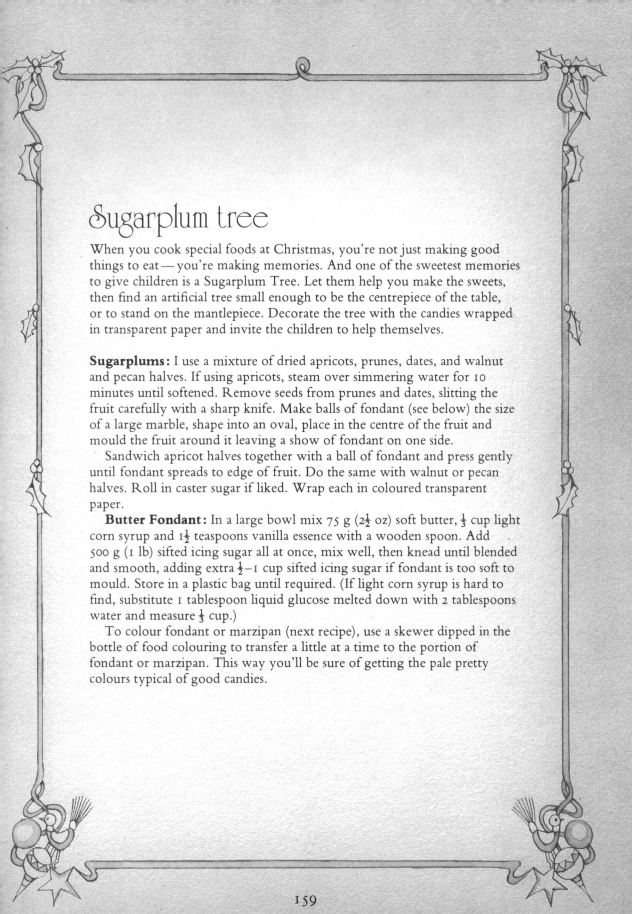

Sugarplum tree

When you cook special foods at Christmas, you're not just making good
things to eat—you're making memories. And one of the sweetest memories
to give children is a Sugarplum Tree. Let them help you make the sweets,
then find an artificial tree small enough to be the centrepiece of the table,
or to stand on the mantlepiece. Decorate the tree with the candies wrapped
in transparent paper and invite the children to help themselves.

Sugarplums: I use a mixture of dried apricots, prunes, dates, and walnut
and pecan halves. If using apricots, steam over simmering water for 10
minutes until softened. Remove seeds from prunes and dates, slitting the
fruit carefully with a sharp knife. Make balls of fondant (see below) the size
of a large marble, shape into an oval, place in the centre of the fruit and
mould the fruit around it leaving a show of fondant on one side.

Sandwich apricot halves together with a ball of fondant and press gently
until fondant spreads to edge of fruit. Do the same with walnut or pecan
halves. Roll in caster sugar if liked. Wrap each in coloured transparent
paper.

Butter Fondant: In a large bowl mix 75 g (2½ oz) soft butter, ⅓ cup light
corn syrup and 1½ teaspoons vanilla essence with a wooden spoon. Add
500 g (1 lb) sifted icing sugar all at once, mix well, then knead until blended
and smooth, adding extra ½–1 cup sifted icing sugar if fondant is too soft to
mould. Store in a plastic bag until required. (If light corn syrup is hard to
find, substitute 1 tablespoon liquid glucose melted down with 2 tablespoons
water and measure ⅓ cup.)

To colour fondant or marzipan (next recipe), use a skewer dipped in the
bottle of food colouring to transfer a little at a time to the portion of
fondant or marzipan. This way you'll be sure of getting the pale pretty
colours typical of good candies.

Marzipan fruits

One of the joys of being a mother is finding your children can do something even better than you can. When I make almond paste for the cake I've always made extra for moulding marzipan fruits, such fun to do. The children love to help.

Now Nina has excelled in the art and makes exquisite miniature fruit that are a joy to behold – and to eat.

Combine 250 g (8 oz) finely ground blanched almonds and 500 g (1 lb) sifted icing sugar in a large bowl. (Save a little icing sugar for rolling out the almond paste and for dusting some of the fruits.) Mix together 2 tablespoons slightly beaten egg white or whole egg, 1 tablespoon sherry or lemon juice, 1 tablespoon brandy, ½ teaspoon almond essence and ½ teaspoon vanilla essence. Add the liquid all at once to the almond and sugar mixture. Knead firmly until thoroughly mixed together and smooth. If too moist, add a little extra icing sugar. Wrap closely in plastic or store in a plastic bag until ready to shape and colour, and do this fairly soon so the marzipan is pliable.

Take small amounts of paste (about a rounded teaspoonful) and roll into balls. For red apples, flatten the balls slightly at either end to make apple shapes. Paint with diluted red food colouring for rosy apples, and insert cloves at either end to represent stem and blossom end.

For green apples, tinting the marzipan throughout gives a better result. Work the green colour into the paste, a tiny drop at a time, kneading firmly and being careful to keep it a nice pale green. Shape, then insert a clove at either end.

For oranges, either knead in colour or paint over, then roll the shape over the surface of a cheese grater for a realistic orange peel. Lemons too are rolled over a grater, but are pointed at each end and painted with light yellow food colouring.

For peaches and apricots, don't flatten the ball as you do for apples and oranges. Instead, point it slightly at one end and mark with the back of a knife down one side to give the typical crease. Tint with diluted food colouring, leave to dry, then roll in sifted icing sugar for 'bloom'. Insert tiny dried leaves from buchu herbal tea at stem end. They look for all the world like miniature peach leaves.

Pears need a little more shaping, but are not difficult. Paint all over with yellow food colour. When quite dry, add a faint blush on one side with diluted red food colour. Add a clove for the stem and another for the blossom end.

Carrots are shaped, then marked horizontally with a knife and painted over in bright orange food colour. For carrot tops, use tiny sprigs of fresh dill.

Peas in the pod need a little fiddling. Roll the tiny peas separately. Make each side of the pod by flattening oval shapes until thin and flat. Press the edges of two flat pieces together to form the pod and place peas inside. Mould to shape. (Use green tinted marzipan rather than paint over.)

Potatoes are perhaps the easiest of all – irregular shapes with 'eyes' made by poking with a skewer, then rolled in cocoa or drinking chocolate powder. Nina sometimes makes a tiny hessian "potato sack" and piles the marzipan potatoes in it.

CHRISTMAS

Christmas time. The frantic to and fro-ing.
Party time. People coming, going.
The search for gifts, the money overspent,
and still the hard reality of mortgages and rent
and the inevitability of next month's bills.
Hangovers and digestive pills.
The weary thought, "It's only once a year, thank God."
Thank God, indeed. We couldn't stand the pace of such
frenetic merriment too often or too much.

This is Christmas? It doesn't have to be,
and peace on earth can start inside of me
if I shut out the world's commercial din,
open my mind to let the Christ Child in.
While music blares in shops ablaze with light,
listen to the message of that dark and silent night.
Exchanging gifts, I must not fail to take
the Gift above all other gifts He gave for our sake,
to hear the strains of carols from afar
and look beyond the tinsel to the Star.

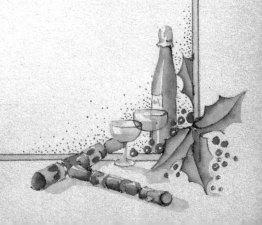

Recipe index

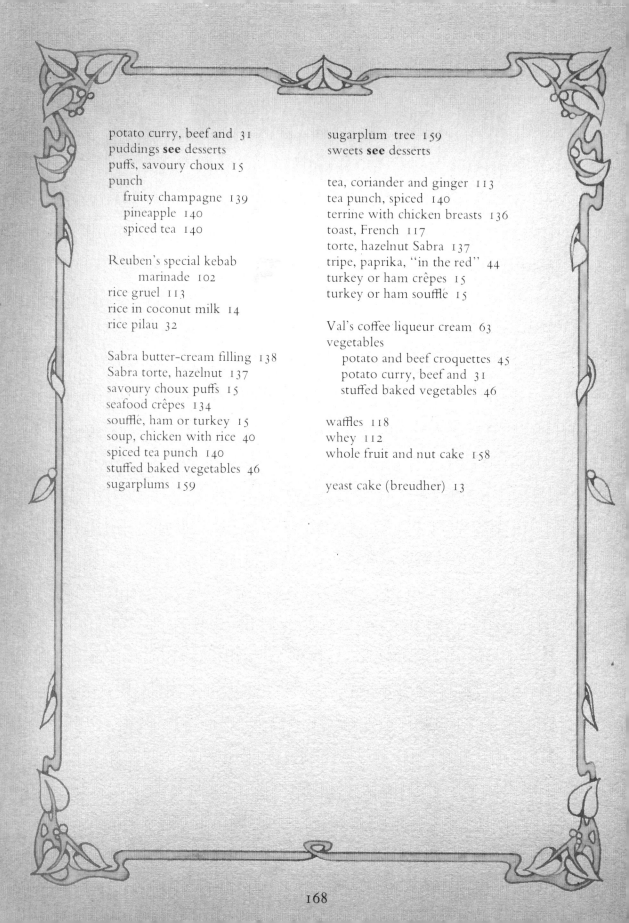